Evolutionary Economics and Social Complexity Science

Volume 13

The Japanese Association for Evolutionary Economics (JAFEE) always has adhered to its original aim of taking an explicit "integrated" approach. This path has been followed steadfastly since the Association's establishment in 1997 and, as well, since the inauguration of our international journal in 2004. We have deployed an agenda encompassing a contemporary array of subjects including but not limited to: foundations of institutional and evolutionary economics, criticism of mainstream views in the social sciences, knowledge and learning in socio-economic life, development and innovation of technologies, transformation of industrial organizations and economic systems, experimental studies in economics, agent-based modeling of socio-economic systems, evolution of the governance structure of firms and other organizations, comparison of dynamically changing institutions of the world, and policy proposals in the transformational process of economic life. In short, our starting point is an "integrative science" of evolutionary and institutional views. Furthermore,we always endeavor to stay abreast of newly established methods such as agent-based modeling, socio/econo-physics, and network analysis as part of our integrative links.

More fundamentally, "evolution" in social science is interpreted as an essential key word, i.e., an integrative and/or communicative link to understand and re-domain various preceding dichotomies in the sciences: ontological or epistemological, subjective or objective, homogeneous or heterogeneous, natural or artificial, selfish or altruistic, individualistic or collective, rational or irrational, axiomatic or psychological-based, causal nexus or cyclic networked, optimal or adaptive, microor macroscopic, deterministic or stochastic, historical or theoretical, mathematical or computational, experimental or empirical, agent-based or socio/econo-physical, institutional or evolutionary, regional or global, and so on. The conventional meanings adhering to various traditional dichotomies may be more or less obsolete, to be replaced with more current ones vis-à-vis contemporary academic trends. Thus we are strongly encouraged to integrate some of the conventional dichotomies.

These attempts are not limited to the field of economic sciences, including management sciences, but also include social science in general. In that way, understanding the social profiles of complex science may then be within our reach. In the meantime, contemporary society appears to be evolving into a newly emerging phase, chiefly characterized by an information and communication technology (ICT) mode of production and a service network system replacing the earlier established factory system with a new one that is suited to actual observations. In the face of these changes we are urgently compelled to explore a set of new properties for a new socio/economic system by implementing new ideas. We thus are keen to look for "integrated principles" common to the above-mentioned dichotomies throughout our serial compilation of publications.We are also encouraged to create a new, broader spectrum for establishing a specific method positively integrated in our own original way.

More information about this series at http://www.springer.com/series/11930

Stephen J. Guastello
Editor

Cognitive Workload and Fatigue in Financial Decision Making

Springer

Editor
Stephen J. Guastello
Psychology Department
Marquette University
Milwaukee, Wisconsin
USA

ISSN 2198-4204 ISSN 2198-4212 (electronic)
Evolutionary Economics and Social Complexity Science
ISBN 978-4-431-56650-2 ISBN 978-4-431-55312-0 (eBook)
DOI 10.1007/978-4-431-55312-0

Springer Tokyo Heidelberg New York Dordrecht London

Softcover re-print of the Hardcover 1st edition 2016

Printed on acid-free paper

Springer Japan KK is part of Springer Science+Business Media (www.springer.com)

Preface

It is perhaps more the rule than the exception that solutions to real-world problems span two or more academic disciplines. From one perspective this book reports the latest insights into the economic principle of bounded rationality, which later led to the understanding of biases in decisions. From another perspective, the book expands our understanding of mental workload and mental fatigue to decisions that simultaneously involve optimization and risk.

The project that is presented in this book actually started with the second perspective and crossed over into the first. The initial ideas came from applications of catastrophe theory that I started in the early 1980s for modeling sudden discontinuities in work performance, such as physical fatigue, physical workload, shift work and industrial production, and occupational accidents and prevention. I found the connections between accident analysis, risk modeling, and the insights that nonlinear dynamics had to offer captivating for a number of years afterwards. The mid-2000s seemed like a good time to rethink mental workload and mental fatigue because technology had changed so much of the work people do for a living. I put together a team of students who were also interested in the topic. We dug into the extant literature and found a rat's nest of entangled and half-explained phenomena. To make matters more interesting, the human factors engineering literature was heading along one path of studying work performance and human–machine interactions, theoretically centered cognitive psychologists were trying to figure out the mechanisms of working memory, and the two camps did not seem to be reading each other very closely. We concluded that nothing was going to be resolved very well unless workload and fatigue processes were studied together in the same experimental tasks, and that two cusp catastrophe models were needed to account for the two processes as they unfolded over time.

The first data collection was launched in the fall of 2009. The long-term plan of the research program was to explore a wide range of cognitive processes with different types of memory demands. Successive experiments pursued both new processes and psychological variables that captured an aspect of the principles of elasticity versus rigidity in human thought processes. After working through a few challenges that involved multitasking, we found our way to financial decision making. Financial decisions were particularly interesting because one decision contained at least two aspects of performance – optimizing and risk taking – and the decision makers were often biased toward one or the other. After that, the rest is not history yet.

I would like to take this opportunity to thank several cohorts of the cognitive workload and fatigue research team for their enthusiastic efforts. Their published works are cited in different chapters throughout this book, and some are co-authors of some of the chapters. I would also like to thank David Pincus for many helpful suggestions to Chapter 7, and J. Barkley Rosser, Jr. and Mohammed H. I. Dore for many fascinating discussions of nonlinear economics over the years. The usual disclaimer applies, of course.

Milwaukee, USA Stephen J. Guastello

Contents

Chapter 1
Bounded Rationality in the Twenty-First Century

Stephen J. Guastello

Abstract This chapter traces the parallel development of the constructs of bounded rationality in economics and cognitive capacity in psychology. Both perspectives led to the study of cognitive biases, the interdisciplinary field of behavioral economics, and artificial intelligence products that solved some of the original problems but created new and similar ones. The role of emotions in ideally rational decision processes also motivated the study of cognitive workload and fatigue in financial decision making, which is the primary focus of this book. The chapter concludes with elementary constructs of nonlinear dynamical systems theory that are intrinsic to the theory of cognitive workload and fatigue that is articulated in Chap. 2.

1.1 Introduction

The construct of *bounded rationality*, introduced by Herbert Simon (1957), made a pivotal impact on economics by challenging the assumption that any and all economic agents were acting in a completely rational fashion whenever they faced a decision. The idea took a long time to catch on, but it eventually became accepted well-enough that decision makers were often in a position of having a limited amount of time available to process enormous amounts of information that could very well lead to rational choices (Rosser and Rosser 2015). Instead, the decision maker needed to *satisfice* – make *a good-enough* decision under the time constraints. In addition to the problems of too much information and not enough time, there is also the problem of complexity of the decision. Complex decisions have multiple interrelated parts, and it is often a challenge to figure out what all the parts should be and how to define the information needed for the appropriate search.

Bounded rationality gave rise to (at least) two important lines of thought. One was the use of computers to extend the rationality of the decision makers. Some of

S.J. Guastello (✉)
Marquette University, Milwaukee, WI, USA
e-mail: Stephen.guastello@marquette.edu

S.J. Guastello (ed.), *Cognitive Workload and Fatigue in Financial Decision Making*, Evolutionary Economics and Social Complexity Science 13,
DOI 10.1007/978-4-431-55312-0_1

the earlier applications involved strategic planning and "war games," and other involved forecasting future states of systems or prices of commodities and securities. There was some sense in the economics and political science communities during the 1950–1990 era that computer power could restore rationality and the "rational man" view of the economic agent. Although information science made important strides in this direction, one is still left with the problem of defining the problem and the nature of the intended decision well enough for programming purposes, acquiring the information necessary to run the inference engine of the program, and to keep the information and artificial intelligence updated to cope with a reality that is naturally in flux (Guastello and Rieke 1994). It is also recognized that automation and artificial intelligence products can shift a lot of the mental workload from humans to computer programs, automation can create new cognitive demands on the human operators because of its processing speed and because automation can become unreliable in the face of novel situations (Sheridan 2002). In fact, trust in automation, complacency with automation, and defining the correct amount of automation are vibrant areas of research in human factors engineering, cognitive science, and related fields (Meyer and Lee 2013).

The other important line of thought involved biases in decision making. Biases are systematic deviations from strict rationality, and were first articulated in a landmark article by Kahneman and Tversky (1979). Since that time other forms of bias have come to the foreground. Ironically, there was the parallel stream of thought developing in cognitive psychology that took the form of cognitive workload and fatigue theories that saw very little cross-over with economic decision making until now. The concept of complexity that was inherent in some of Simon's scenarios for bounded rationality (Simon 1962/2004; Faggini and Vinci 2010; Rosser and Rosser 2015) did not extend to workload and fatigue dynamics. The next sections of this chapter examine decision structures in greater detail, with emphasis on the structures that are examined in depth here. From there we examine biases in bit more detail, and then examine some constructs that are needed for studying cognitive workload and fatigue and their impact on decision results, which do unfold indeed over time.

1.1.1 Types of Decisions

The extended experiment and analysis in this project are confined to apparently simple optimizing decisions. If one looks closely enough, "simple" can become complex quickly enough, and optimizing components can be found within many forms of non-optimizing decisions.

1.1.1.1 Optimizing Decisions

Given a set of possible choices, which one will produce the best results? If we have a situation in which there are defined options and rational behavior, optimal outcomes (Max [O]), and odds of an outcome coming to fruition (Pr[O]), a strictly rational decision takes the form:

$$E[O] = Max[O] \times Pr[O] \tag{1.1}$$

where $E[O]$ is the expected outcome.

The concept represented in Eq. 1.1 surfaced in psychology with cognitive learning theory (Tolman 1932). The principle was that the rat *knows where* the cheese is. The idea of a rat knowing anything ran counter to the tenets of behaviorism as it existed at the time, which assumed nothing whatsoever about mental processes or structures. If a construct could not be observed or measured objectively, it did not exist. Although this criterion might appear overly stringent, if not absurd, today, it was very necessary a century ago because several strains of psychological theory at the time were predicated on assumptions of mental processes that could not be observed or verified one way or the other. It was not until much later that behavioral methods could cross over to the cognitive domains in which the unseen mental processes could be studied from the vantage point of behavioral outcomes.

For similar reasons, the idea that a rat knew where anything was located also ran counter to strict behaviorism because one would have to assume that invisible cognitive structures existed. Tolman's experiments were designed to consider the possibility that such structures did exist, and he gave them the name *cognitive maps.* Cognitive maps are mental representations of a physical environment that are embodied in the individual and which the individual uses to solve problems concerning the location of objects or one's personal location in space and how to move to another location. In the most pointed experiments, Tolman would first allow his rats to explore a radial maze without any reward. A radial maze has several walkways organized in a circle that all converge on a central area in the middle. He would then place cheese of different amounts in different fingers of the radial maze, and the fingers of the maze would be used at varying probabilities. The rat would be allowed to enter the maze from any of the opening, would run toward the middle, then take whatever left or right turns were necessary to go to the maze finger the had the greatest likelihood of containing the most cheese, as expressed by Eq. 1.1. If there was no cheese in that target space, the rat would return and go to the second most likely location, and so on. If the rat entered the maze from different points, and the location of maximum cheese was the same in each case, the rat would need to make a different set of left or right turns to reach the cheese. Because the rat was able to do so, the conclusion was that the rat had a cognitive map of the maze. In an optimizing choice decision, the decision maker would mentally construct Eq. 1.1 for each option. The option that produces the best $E[O]$ would be the option of choice.

Sources of complexity in optimizing decisions include the number of options, costs to participate (what securities brokers would call *front-end load*), and the reconnaissance and preparation work needed to determine what the valances and probabilities actually area. The latter make the difference between "risk" and "uncertainty" in the formal sense (Rosser and Rosser 2015), although it would be fair to say that engaging in a decision that involves a lot of uncertainty is a risky proposition in the more conventional use of the word. Nonetheless, if one does not *know* the *Pr*[*O*], one is forced to guess at it somehow. *Overconfidence bias* occurs when the individual overestimates the odds of success.

Optimization also occurs in game-theoretical decisions. All agents try to maximize their own outcomes, but the valences or utilities for any one agent depend on the options selected by other agents. Complexity in this context would arise from the number of agents, number of options, and differences between the utilities to the collective and utilities to the individual. Another source of complexity arises from one-shot exchanges and evolutionarily stable states; the latter cannot be predicted from the former except under very restrictive assumptions.

In many cases, the utilities of a situation can be stated simply as profits from a financial exchange. Complications arise when multiple and conflicting utilities could exist. For instance, agents may find themselves choosing between a financial gain and a social cost, or a social good and a financial compromise (Bruno 2010). Some gains or costs could be short term while others take longer to realize, thus there is another form of trade-off or complexity (Gärling et al. 2009). Within an organization, managers often need to choose between production goals and safety (Reason 1997) or between production quantity, product quality, and investing in human resources (Borges and Guastello 1998). As another example, some business organizations have made the questionable decision to increase short-term profitability by reducing research and development "overhead," thereby hampering the organization's adaptive capability in the longer term.

1.1.1.2 Non-optimizing Decisions

Some of the more prevalent forms of non-optimizing decisions include forecasting, planning a future state, creative thinking, and insight and pattern recognition (Guastello 2014). All four types have numerous opportunities for complexity and embedded optimizing.

One type of forecasting involves the prediction of numerical values, such as prices of securities, based on previous trends. These are the computerized remedies for bounded rationality that are susceptible to the limitations of artificial intelligence systems that were mentioned earlier. Forecasting problems can become more complex and predictions can become more uncertain if the time series is non-stationary, meaning that the computational rules that fit one part of the time series do not generalize to another segment of the time series. Forecasters are thus compelled to state that the forecasts will occur as predicted if the underlying system does not change in the ensuing time horizon. Another source of complexity, and an opportunity for optimizing comes with the choice of the mathematical or statistical model that one uses. It is possible to analyze a time series of data with a few different models, find the model that fits the data best, and adopt the model as an optimized solution. It is also possible to have two models that are close to equal in their accuracy levels, but either make very different forecasts about the future or contain elements that are qualitatively different in their information content. "Optimal" in these cases could mean that one should use both models or find another modal that produces less ambiguous results and thus simplifies the process of interpretation.

Planning future states of a system, or making action plans involve complexity from a few different sources. If the system has many interacting elements, it could self-organize in more than one way. There might be multiple paths to a goal, or multiple end states to reconcile. Furthermore, if there are slight differences in initial conditions, very different end states could emerge once all the agents have interacted (randomly or otherwise) over an extended period of time. It is possible to compute such outcomes using techniques such as agent-based models or cellular automata (Epstein and Axtell 1996). In fact, that is how complexity theory got its name: There were too many agents, interactions, and possible outcomes leading to more interactions to calculate the system states on the basis of each possibility. Agent-based modeling and related techniques were devised to meet this computational challenge. The limitations of artificial intelligence still apply: The assumptions about the agents' behavior, and probabilities of doing one thing or another need to be drawn from real world observation, or else the predictions for the virtual world might not resemble reality at all (Frantz and Carley 2009).

Creative thinking is fundamentally different from optimizing, at least at the start of a thought process. Optimizing is *convergent*, meaning that the goal is to identify the correct answer or the best answer. Creative thinking is *divergent*, meaning that the goal is to generate many possible answers and ideas. One then moves forward to arranging the idea elements in multiple ways to solve a problem. Optimizing sets in eventually when one must decide which ideas have the greatest expected utility relative to how much they will cost to implement. Research and development laboratories make such decisions regularly. They have multiple ideas and projects that they could pursue, but the agents need to evaluate which ones would produce the best outcomes, and by choosing some options forego the opportunity to work on other options (Sternberg and Lubart 1991).

Insights are suddenly occurring thoughts that often take the form of solutions to a problem or phase shifts in the understanding of a situation. Insights could arise during a creative thinking process, but they are not necessarily limited to creative thinking. Insights can be found in other forms of situation awareness, and they occur in psychotherapy to both the therapist and client. At first, agents do not see a pattern, then suddenly they do see one. Alternatively, they could be working under the assumption that one pattern is in effect, but enough information arrives to change the interpretation of the environment (Arecchi 2011). Changing the interpretation often leads to a change in the action plan. Many types of information systems are designed to facilitate situation awareness by providing the right amount of information of the right content at the right time (Endsley et al. 2003). One might anticipate that the word "situation" could apply so broadly that any level of complexity could be involved. The idea of *right* amounts, content, and timing involves optimization in the system design process. If the (automation) system is going to be usable, it cannot overwhelm the agents' boundaries on rationality. By the same token, Ashby's (1956) law of requisite variety also applies: A controller must be at least as complex as the system it intends to control.

Finally for this group of decision types, on can ask what happens if the situation is ambiguous? There is another level of optimization that occurs when trying to answer: What is gained by assuming one interpretation versus another? What are the costs of being wrong either way? Sometimes the latter two questions can be answered fairly well, and at other times not so well.

1.1.1.3 Biases in Decisions

Financial decisions are known to be subject to several forms of bias such as the reflection effect, overweighting certainty (Kahneman and Tversky 1979), overconfidence (Fisher and Statman 2000; Thierry 2007) and various types of statistical forecasting errors (Elliott and Timmermann 2008; Friesen and Weller 2005; Lowenstein 2006). The reflection effect occurs when a decision maker places undue weight on costs and potential losses. In a strictly rational situation, $1000 gained is no different from $1000 lost or spent; the amount is still $1000. Psychologically however, $1000 lost is a bigger amount than the $1000 gained. The reflection effect is essentially loss aversion. Professional investors do minimize risk by other means, such as portfolio management and option trading, but those strategies fall outside the scope of the phenomena studied in the experiment here.

Overweighting certainty occurs when the decision maker selects the option that does not produce the greatest expected utility, but instead selects the option that has the highest probability of a positive payoff of a lesser amount. Usually there is a balance that the individual will strike between something assured and the risk associated with getting something better than what the surest option has to offer. This balance is sometimes known as a *risk profile*. Overconfidence and forecasting errors were explained earlier.

The foregoing challenges to rationality result in questionable levels of success for mutual fund and hedge fund managers, to the extent that some analysts claim that some fund managers are not doing much better than taking a random walk through the investment opportunities (Amenc et al. 2004; Edwards and Caglayan 2001; Géhin 2003; Lowenstein 2006). The trepidations of automation have been mentioned already, but the twenty-first Century version of the problem could make the random walk look attractive. Automated trading has produced flash-crashes where a market could plummet and recover within a half hour or less (Wilkins and Dragos 2013). Because the automation that any particular agent might use is used in an environment that is dominated by other agents' automation, agents can no longer predict markets if they ever could. They can only predict how *other* agents and their automation systems would respond. Thus if one agent's program is selling at a high volume or rate of speed and producing price drops, the other programs would detect this activity and respond in kind. Humans can intervene, however, if they catch the problem and react quickly enough.

1.1.2 Emotion, Motivation, and Stress

A strictly rational agent that is optimizing like Tolman's rats knew how to do would not be influenced by emotional attachments to a security or a piece of cheese. Humans can become attached to a particular investment, social utility, or strategic plan in dysfunctional ways. In traditional thinking, the influence of emotions would be reason enough to declare that the "rational man" does not exist, and perhaps a new type of boundary to rationality should be acknowledged. (Keynes 1965) recognized that such *animal spirits* not only exist, but could spread (Gomes 2015). Psychologists and behavioral economists have been studying the role of emotions and concluding in some cases that emotions can enhance decision quality instead of detracting from it, which is the usual assumption (Blanchette 2014; Wilhelms and Reyna 2015). When faced with ambiguous circumstances that cannot be resolved with available information, a decision makers needs to rely on intuition, "gut instincts" or "the little voices in their heads." All other things being equal, experts in a technical area often have better-developed instincts than novices.

If one thinks about the issue of emotions a bit more carefully, it makes good sense that emotions can enhance rather than hinder. It is now well-accepted that the neurocognitive foundations of motivation and emotion are the same. The difference lies in the interpretation of the psychological events or the individuals' interpretation of their own experience. Both start with physiological arousal, which is induced by situational events or constraints (McClelland et al. 1953). When arousal is combined with positive or negative situational events and a relative unawareness that the event is happening, the individual experiences clear positive and negative emotions (Schachter and Singer 1962). Later research has determined that there are specific emotions that are universally (cross-culturally) recognized through facial expressions (Schels et al. 2009). Most contemporary human languages have substantial vocabularies for finer shades of emotion, and there is now a psychological concept of emotional intelligence (EI in the chapters that follow) that defines a person's ability to identify and distinguish emotions and act upon them in a constructive manner (Mayer and Salovey 1997). EI is part of the cognitive workload and fatigue theory that is developed in the chapters that follow.

A motivation is goal-directed. In the prototype situation, a person can construct an action plan to reach one or more goals. The work of McClelland et al. (1953) bifurcated into studies of emotion, as just described, and motivation. They determined that previous psychological studies of "emotional needs" could organize the so-called needs into three distinct social expressions – achievement, affiliation, and power. A digression into these three forms is beyond the scope of the present research. It is relevant for present purposes, however, that people who might be called "greedy" in some contexts are reframed by their employers in financial institutions are "high-achievers" (Gärling et al. 2009).

A person who is motivated for something, however, will not only construct action plans, but also recognize opportunities in the environment – what other psychologists have called *affordances* (Gibson 1979) – that could serve the prevailing motivations. Preoccupation with the goals or emotions can induce biases toward one decision outcome or another that are inconsistent with true rationality. In other words, wishful thinking can be hazardous, particularly for impulsive individuals. Impulsivity is another variable is part of the cognitive workload and fatigue model that is developed in the next two chapters.

One can put the three-way connections between emotion, motivation, and decision-making together into what some researchers call dual-process theory (Van Duijvendoorde et al. 2015). One process is the activation of mental schemata to pursue a goal, and the other is the emotional control process. The latter is part of EI. The dual-process concept also stems from the neurological mechanisms of activation and inhibition. The dual process is not well understood, especially when behavioral outcomes are involved. Nonetheless, the prefix "neuro-," appearing in words such as "neuroeconomics," "neurocognitive," or "neuro-this-that-or-the other," have become common. With that thought in mind, the research that is captured in the following chapters makes no pretense of neuro-anything except to acknowledge that neurological connections with cognitive events are being studied vigorously by others, and comprehensive explanations of "biopsychosocial" events are starting to take form.

1.1.3 Channel Capacity

When Simon's bounded rationality fought its way into the perspectives of economists, there was a psychological counterpart, the study of cognitive capacity, that was developing at the same time. Not surprisingly, there was little connection between psychology and economics until the landmark article by Kahneman and Tversky (1979). Their work articulated some fundamental types of cognitive biases, and it soon met with contributions by other economists whose work evolved into the distinctive sub-discipline of behavioral economics (Rosser and Rosser 2015). Behavioral economics is not confined to the classical notions of behaviorism that Tolman revolted against, but includes a much broader range of ideas that represent a cross-over between economics and psychology.

The psychological stream started with Broadbent (1958) who introduced the concepts of channel capacity and attentional filtering. The concept of channel capacity is easier to explain if we assume (temporarily) that there is a rigid fixed upper limit to the human mental channel capacity. The total capacity may be divided among primary, secondary, and even tertiary tasks or channels, where mental efforts are allocated among the tasks. The allocation function is thought to function like a time-sharing computer; this is a metaphor that persisted from the early 1950s to the mid-1980s when personal computers were slowing becoming the dominant medium of computer use. The mainframe would work on jobs that were submitted by many users at the same time. A certain amount of time would be allocated to processing each person's job. Run times for a job on a mainframe were enormously faster after midnight when most system users were sleeping instead of working. The analogy to human information was process ran as follows: If a person's total channel capacity was really 10 bits per second, and the primary task only required 6 bits per second, then 4 bits per second were left over for the secondary task. If the secondary task did not require the full 4 bits, then some small amount was left over for a tertiary task (Kantowitz 1985). One should be aware, however, that (a) the fixed capacity model has given way to the idea that cognitive capacity is actually variable; (b) the total capacity is roughly distributed between modality of input, thought and actions, such as visual processing, auditory processing, and psychomotor response (Baddeley 2003; Wickens 2002); and (c) any notions of bits per second that one might see in older studies are highly relative to the task, if not also the people performing it, and not generalizable as a metric for human cognitive processing.

The remainder of the book is concerned with the behavioral outcomes of cognitive workload and fatigue, their most proximal dynamics, and behavioral effects over time. Cognitive workload is a form of stress, which, in extenuating conditions produces emotional reactions that are mostly unwanted. Fatigue is both a consequence of workload, but also extended time on task. Both processes work together to produce performance decrements. The goal of explaining the transition between the mental state and performance on decision tasks, and the role of external events on the mental state, has challenged psychological researchers, particularly in the specialties of human factors engineering and ergonomics, for the better part of a century. The exposition of the central issues is reserved for Chap. 2. For present purposes, however, the connection between emotions and biases in financial decisions has only been extended to stress issues in very limited ways. The present effort proceeds from the other perspective, that of cognitive workload and fatigue, which addresses a broad range of cognitive demands. The evolving theory of those cognitive processes is now extended to financial decisions.

1.1.4 Nonlinear Dynamics

In spite of the decades of research of cognitive workload, channel capacity and fatigue, theoretical clarity has been seriously limited by experiments that have adopted conventional experimental designs. The nonlinear dynamical systems (NDS) approach involves observing changes in performance over time and characterizes those changes with dynamical models that do not assume that all forms of change are similar in origin or are produced in the same way. In NDS theory and its broad range of applications, there are several distinct concepts of temporal change that have enlightened many phenomena in psychology (Guastello 2009; Gärling et al. 2009) and economics (Dore and Rosser 2007; Rosser 2000, 2004). Thus the final section of this chapter introduces the constructs from nonlinear dynamics that are used, often in combination, in the analyses and interpretations appearing in later chapters. Other NDS constructs are explained in later chapters as they are needed.

1.1.4.1 Attractors and Bifurcations

The structures previously known as "equilibria" are now understood as one of several basic forms of attractor. An attractor is a piece of space. When an object enters, it does not exist unless a substantial force is applied to it. The simplest attractor is the *fixed point*. Oscillators, also known as *limit cycles*, are another type of attractor. They can be simple oscillators, or dampened to a fixed point by means of a *control parameter*. They can also be perturbed in the opposite direction to become *aperiodic oscillators*. There is a gradual transition from aperiodic attractors to chaotic attractors.

Repellors are like attractors, but they work backwards. Objects that veer too close to them are pushed outward and can go anywhere, so long as they go away. This property of an indeterminable final outcome is what makes repellors unstable. Fixed points and oscillators, in contrast, are stable. Chaotic attractors (described below) are also stable in spite of their popular association with unpredictability.

A *saddle* has mixed properties of an attractor and a repellor. Objects are drawn to it, but are pushed away once they arrive. A saddle is also unstable.

Bifurcations are splits in a dynamic field that can occur when an attractor changes from one type to another, or where different dynamics are occurring in juxtaposing pieces of space. Bifurcations can be as simple as a single point, or they may involve trajectories and patterns of instability that can become very complex.

Much of the empirical work that appears in the next few chapters involves a particular configuration of fixed point attractors, a bifurcation, a saddle, and a repellor. When these elements are assembled in the right way, they form a cusp catastrophe, which is a model for describing and predicting sudden change between two stable states.

1.1.4.2 Chaos and Fractal Dimensions

The essence of chaos is that seemingly random events can actually be explained by simple deterministic processes or equations (Kaplan and Glass 1995; Sprott 2003). Chaos has three hallmark properties: sensitivity to initial conditions, boundedness, and unpredictability.

Sensitivity to initial conditions means that two points can start by being arbitrarily close together, but as the same function continues to iterate for both of them, the two points become increasingly further apart; this is the well-known *butterfly effect*. *Boundedness* means that, in spite of the volatility of the measurement being observed, the values of the measurement stay within a fixed range. *Unpredictability* is actually a matter of degree and sometimes an overstatement, depending on the context. What actually occurs is that it becomes increasingly difficult to predict a point from a previous one as the time interval becomes larger, unless we know the nonlinear function in advance, which is seldom the case. *Information loss* occurs when predictability drops sharply over time.

In light of the large number of known chaotic systems, researchers in applied contexts usually focus on the generic properties of chaos and how it might be differentiated from other nonlinear dynamics. One such metric for doing so is the *fractal dimension*, which may also serve as a measure of complexity. A fractal is a geometric structure that repeats its shape at different levels of scale; one can zoom in on a portion of the shape and see the whole shape within the smaller space. Fractals have fractional dimensionality, meaning that they exist between lines and planes or between planes and closed cubes.

The test for chaos is currently done primarily with the *Lyapunov exponent*, which measures the amount of turbulence in a time series. It is calculated from sequential differences in values of the behavioral measurement (time series variable) and the extent to which the differences expand and contract. Larger values indicate faster information loss in a system as one attempts to predict the state of the system at many points into the future. The constructs of chaos, fractal dimensions, and Lyapunov exponents are used in Chap. 7 in which these constructs are combined with others to produce risk-optimization profiles for a sequence of decisions made by an agent or a team.

References

Amenc, N., Curtis, S., & Martellini, L. (2004). *The alpha and omega of hedge fund performance measurement*. Lille: EDHEC Risk and Asset Management Research Centre. Retrieved December 15, 2011, from http://www.edhecrisk.com/performance_and_style_analysis/Hendge_funds_performance

Arecchi, F. T. (2011). Phenomenology of consciousness: From apprehension to judgment. *Nonlinear Dynamics, Psychology, and Life Sciences, 15*, 359–376.

Ashby, W. R. (1956). *Introduction to cybernetics*. New York: Wiley.

Baddeley, A. (2003). Working memory: Looking back and looking forward. *Nature Reviews Neuroscience, 4*, 829–839.

Bruno, S. (2010). Optimization and "thoughtful conjecturing" as principles of analytical guidance in social decision making. In C. P. Vinci (Ed.), *Decision theory and choices: A complexity approach*. New York: Springer.

Blanchette, I. (Ed.). (2014). *Emotion and reasoning*. New York: Psychology Press.

Borges, L. A. J., & Guastello, S. J. (1998). Chaos theory applied to TQM: A survey. In W. L. Baker (Ed.), *Proceedings of the 52nd annual quality congress* (pp. 578–585). Philadelphia: American Society for Quality Control.

Broadbent, D. E. (1958). *Perception and communication*. Elmsford: Pergamon Press.

Dore, M. H. I., & Rosser, J. B., Jr. (2007). Do nonlinear dynamics in economics amount to a Kuhnian paradigm? *Nonlinear Dynamics, Psychology, and Life Sciences, 11*, 119–148.

Edwards, F. R., & Caglayan, M. O. (2001). Hedge fund performance and manager skill. *Journal of Futures Markets, 21*, 1003–1028.
Elliott, G., & Timmermann, A. (2008). Economic forecasting. *Journal of Economic Literature, 46*, 3–56.
Endsley, M. R., Bolté, B., & Jones, D. G. (2003). *Designing for situation awareness: An approach to user-centered design*. Boca Raton: CRC Press.
Epstein, J. M., & Axtell, R. (1996). *Growing artificial societies: Social science from the bottom up*. Cambridge, MA: MIT Press.
Faggini, M., & Vinci, C. P. (Eds.). (2010). *Decision theory and choices: A complexity approach*. New York: Springer.
Fisher, K. L., & Statman, M. (2000). Cognitive biases in market forecasts. *Journal of Portfolio Management, Fall*, 1–10.
Frantz, T. L., & Carley, K. M. (2009). Agent-based modeling within a dynamic network. In S. J. Guastello, M. Koopmans, & D. Pincus (Eds.), *Chaos and complexity in psychology: The theory of nonlinear dynamical systems* (pp. 475–505). New York: Cambridge University Press.
Friesen, G. C., & Weller, P. (2005). *Quantifying cognitive biases in analyst earnings forecasts*. Lincoln: University of Nebraska Finance Department. Retrieved December 15, 2011, from http://digicalcommons.unl.edu/financefacpub/23
Gärling, T., Kirchler, E., Lewis, A., & van Raaij, F. (2009). Psychology, financial decision making, and financial crises. *Psychological Science in the Public Interest, 10*, 1–47.
Géhin, W. (2003). *Hedge fund performance*. Lille: EDHEC Risk and Asset Management Research Centre. Retrieved December 15, 2011, from http://www.edhec-risk.com/performance_and_style_analysis/Hendge_funds_performance
Gibson, J. J. (1979). *The ecological approach to visual perception*. Boston: Houghton Mifflin.
Gomes, O. (2015). A model of animal spirits via sentiment spreading. *Nonlinear Dynamics, Psychology, and Life Sciences, 19*, 313–343.
Guastello, S. J. (2009). Chaos as a psychological construct: Historical roots, principal findings, and current growth directions. *Nonlinear Dynamics, Psychology, and Life Sciences, 13*, 289–310.
Guastello, S. J. (2014). *Human factors engineering and ergonomics: A systems approach*. Boca Raton: CRC Press.
Guastello, S. J., & Rieke, M. L. (1994). Computer–based test interpretations as expert systems: Validity and viewpoints from artificial intelligence theory. *Computers in Human Behavior, 4*, 435–495.
Kahneman, D., & Tversky, A. (1979). Prospect theory: An analysis of decision under risk. *Econometrica, 47*, 253–291.
Kantowitz, B. H. (1985). Channels and stages in human information processing: A limited analysis of theory and methodology. *Journal of Mathematical Psychology, 29*, 135–174.
Kaplan, D., & Glass, L. (1995). *Understanding nonlinear dynamics*. New York: Springer.
Keynes, J. M. (1965). *General theory of employment, interest, and money* (2nd ed.). New York: Harcourt Brace.
Lowenstein, L. (2006). Search for rational investors in a perfect storm: A behavioral perspective. *The Journal of Behavioral Finance, 7*, 66–74.
Mayer, J. D., & Salovey, P. (1997). What is emotional intelligence? In P. Salovey & D. Sluyter (Eds.), *Emotional development and emotional intelligence: Educational implications* (pp. 3–34). New York: Basic Books.
McClelland, D. C., Atkinson, J. W., Clark, R. A., & Lowell, E. L. (1953). *The achievement motive*. New York: Appleton-Century-Croft.
Meyer, J., & Lee, J. D. (2013). Trust, reliance, and compliance. In *The Oxford handbook of cognitive engineering* (pp. 109–124). New York: Oxford University Press.
Reason, J. (1997). *Managing the risks of organizational accidents*. Brookfield: Ashgate.
Rosser, J. B., Jr. (2000). *From catastrophe to chaos: A general theory of economic discontinuities* (2nd ed.). Norwell: Kluwer Academic Publishers.
Rosser, J. B., Jr. (Ed.). (2004). *Complexity in economics*. Cheltenham: Edward Elgar.

Rosser, J. B., Jr., & Rosser, M. V. (2015). Complexity and behavioral economics. *Nonlinear Dynamics, Psychology, and Life Sciences, 19*, 201–226.

Schachter, S., & Singer, J. (1962). Cognitive, social, and physiological determinants of emotional state. *Psychological Review, 69*, 379–399.

Schels, M., Thiel, C., Schwenker, F., & Palm, G. (2009). Classifier fusion applied to facial expression recognition: An experimental comparison. In H. Ritter, G. Sagerer, R. Dillmann, & M. Buss (Eds.), *Human centered robot systems: Cognition, interaction, technology* (pp. 121–130). New York: Springer.

Sheridan, T. B. (2002). *Humans and automation: System design and research issues*. New York: Wiley.

Simon, H. A. (1957). *Administrative behavior* (2nd ed.). Totowa: Littlefield Adams.

Simon, H. A. (1962/2004). The architecture of complexity. *Proceedings of the American Philosophical Society, 106*, 467–482. Reprinted in J. B. Rosser, Jr. (Ed.), *Complexity in economics*. Cheltenham: Edward Elgar.

Sprott, J. C. (2003). *Chaos and time-series analysis*. New York: Oxford.

Sternberg, R. J., & Lubart, T. I. (1991). An investment theory of creativity and its development. *Human Development, 34*, 1–31.

Thierry, B.-H. (2007). Rules of thumb and real option decision biases for optimally imperfect decisions: A simulation-based exploration. *Investment Management and Financial Innovations, 4*, 105–118.

Tolman, E. C. (1932). *Purposive behavior in animals and man*. New York: Century.

Van Duijvendoorde, A. C. K., Jansen, B. R. J., & Huizenga, H. M. (2015). Risky choice from childhood to adulthood: Change in decision strategies, affect, and control. In E. A. Wilhelms & V. F. Reyna (Eds.), *Neuroeconomics, judgment, and decision making* (pp. 203–218). New York: Psychology Press.

Wickens, C. D. (2002). Multiple resources and performance prediction. *Theoretical Issues in Ergonomics Science, 3*, 159–177.

Wilhelms, E. A., & Reyna, V. F. (Eds.). (2015). *Neuroeconomics, judgment, and decision making*. New York: Psychology Press.

Wilkins, I., & Dragos, B. (2013). *Destructive destruction? An ecological study of high frequency trading*. Retrieved February 16, 2013, from http://www.metamute.org/

Chapter 2
Theoretical Issues in Cognitive Workload and Fatigue

Stephen J. Guastello

Abstract This chapter presents the elementary concepts of stress and then focuses to the more specific issues of cognitive workload and fatigue and their role in the nonlinear dynamical systems theory that is the central concern for this book. The roles of working memory and individual differences in cognitive processes are outlined. The chapter culminates in a pair of cusp catastrophe models for cognitive workload and fatigue. The models feature prominent constructs of elasticity versus rigidity in the context of workload and compensatory abilities in the context of fatigue. Previous research on the pair of models is summarized, and the models are adapted with new provisions for basic optimizing and risk taking decisions that are part of many economically relevant decisions.

2.1 Nature and Type of Stress

In the classical definition, stress is the nonspecific reaction of an organism to any environmental demand (Quick and Quick 1984; Selye 1976). This definition is intentionally broad, indicating that any form of stimulation constitutes stress. Both desirable and undesirable events can produce stress (Holmes and Rahe 1967), and that what is negative or undesirable is really a matter of degree and interpretation. The association that is commonly made between stress and negative valence is likely the result of researchers studying particular types of experience that people find distressing.

The physiological dynamics of stress are rooted in the two subdivisions of the autonomic nervous system. The sympathetic nervous system is responsible for bodily arousal when it is activated. Once sufficient energy has been expended, the parasympathetic nervous system is activated and the body relaxes; relaxation is a physiologically active process, not a passive process. Stress reactions occur when sympathetic nervous system arousal is frequent, but there is no opportunity to

S.J. Guastello (✉)
Marquette University, Milwaukee, WI, USA
e-mail: Stephen.guastello@marquette.edu

S.J. Guastello (ed.), *Cognitive Workload and Fatigue in Financial Decision Making*, Evolutionary Economics and Social Complexity Science 13,
DOI 10.1007/978-4-431-55312-0_2

expend energy at the moment when it is necessary to do so, thus prolonged arousal results. Exercise programs are thus frequently recommended to people who need to alleviate the effects of stress in their lives (Zwerling et al. 1997).

There are many types of stress that a person can experience. Although they have common results on the person, it is convenient to classify them according to their sources because the goal is, ultimately, to reduce unnecessary stress both in the workplace and in one's personal life. The four broad categories are, therefore, physical stressors, social stressors, and speed and load stress, and disregulation due to irregular work schedules. Physical stressors include toxins, extreme temperatures, and other environmental discomforts. Social stressors would include job insecurity and other work-related problems, new job assignments, changes in family life patterns, illnesses, deaths, vacations, and holidays. Dysregulation stressors involve disruptions of eating and sleeping patterns, or missing meals or sleep; they are connected to fatigue-related problems that arise from prolonged time on task.

Performance deficits caused by cognitive workload and cognitive fatigue arise from different but related origins. Working memory in particular plays a pivotal role in moderating cognitive workload and fatigue. The basic functions of working memory are explained next, and are followed by some important points about speed and load stress, fatigue, and the modeling strategy for studying the two problems.

2.1.1 Working Memory

Cognitive workload and fatigue are often conflated in real work environments and difficult to separate (Ackerman 2011; Hancock 2013; Hancock and Desmond 2001; Matthews et al. 2012). As workload increases, performance decreases and fatigue becomes more likely; as more time is spent on the task, fatigue sets in pushing performance downward, but learning or momentum effects push performance in a positive direction. The trends are captured in Fig. 2.1.

It has been possible, however, to deconstruct the impact of workload and fatigue on performance with the use of two cusp catastrophe models, one for workload and one for fatigue, and a time series experimental design that is sufficiently complex for separating the two phenomena (Guastello 2013; Guastello et al. 2012a, b, 2013a, 2014b, 2015a). The studies that have used this strategy explored the applicability of the two models in a range of occupationally relevant tasks. They have also explored numerous psychological constructs related to elasticity and compensatory abilities, which proceed from the theory of working memory. The present application to financial decision making is particularly interesting because it involves two parameters of performance, optimizing and risk tasking.

The connected but distinct nature of workload and fatigue deficits are inherent in the cognitive structure of working memory. Working memory is "assumed to be a hierarchical system involving short-term memory, representational components, plus a general executive attentional component" (Kane and Engle 2002, p. 638).

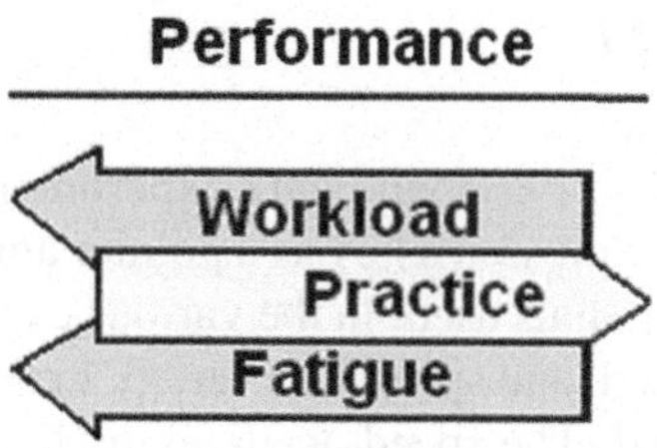

Fig. 2.1 Bi-directional influences of workload and time on task on performance (Reprinted from Guastello et al. (2014c, p. 306) with permission of the Society for Chaos Theory in Psychology & Life Sciences)

Working memory capacity is considerably less than the total long-term memory storage space. Facts, rules, and experiences are called out of long-term memory by the working memory they need to be used. Sometimes multiple sets of facts and rules are called up if the operator is trying to perform two tasks at once (multitasking).

The representational components are workspace modules that are associated with specific types of memory and cognitive functioning (Logie 2011). The executive function recruits workspaces and the functions needed to perform a task. The executive function also maintains the focus of attention. When we tell someone, "Watch what you're doing!" we are recommending a re-engagement of the executive function, which might have lapsed due to fatigue or distraction. Whereas human factors engineers examine properties of tasks that result in performance stability or decline under different types of load conditions, cognitive psychologists investigate the structure and function of working memory itself (Baddeley 2003).

The limits to our ability to process information at a given moment is called *channel capacity*, which is essentially the main boundary in "bounded rationality." Baddeley (2003) identified two basic channels in the 1970s, known as the phonological loop (basically auditory) and the visuospatial sketchpad (basically visual). There are other channels, in addition, however, such as psychomotor response; there are only so many things a person can do with one hand at a particular moment. The total available working memory capacity is likely to be an emergent result of the working memory components that are required by a particular task (Logie 2011). For more demanding tasks, the domain-general function of attentional control supplements the domain-specific resources. Furthermore, memory and processing are two different functions with different capacities, although they normally operate together to varying degrees.

All other things being equal, two tasks are less likely to incur a bottleneck in cognitive processing if they require different perceptual, cognitive, or motor resources rather than the same resources (Wickens 2002, 2008). The present study of financial decisions only involves a single task. The nuance, however, relative to the dual task literature, is that there are two conjoint cognitive processes involved, optimizing and risk taking, within the same decision set. To our knowledge, workload and fatigue have not been studied with cognitive processes configured in this manner before.

2.1.2 Speed and Load

The participants in Conrad's (1951) landmark experiment were engaged in a clock-watching task in which they pressed a key as a pointer approached the 12:00 or 6:00 position on any of the clock dials used. In the various experimental conditions, two, three, or four dials were used, and speed was varied. Errors increased as the product of speed and load increased. The speed-accuracy trade-off (Kantowitz and Sorkin 1983) is another landmark that captures the importance of critical points: People can increase their work speed without making more mistakes, but only up to a critical point. After the critical point the error rates increase dramatically. The engineering strategy would be to set the work pace to the point located just before the sharp increase in errors occurs.

Hancock and Warm (1989) re-examined the inverse-U function that was first introduced by Yerkes and Dodson (1908) that specifies that there is an optimal level of arousal associated with work performance. Hancock and Warm concluded that the inverse-U is actually flat at the top (Fig. 2.2). People maintain a steady level of performance in the neighborhood of the optimal point. When workload exceeds the normal comfort zone in either direction, they engage in coping strategies to stretch their zone. Coping strategies could include off-loading complicated or time-sinking tasks to other people or delaying them until another time, ignoring social interactions that are irrelevant to the task, using automatic thinking processes and less executive control, and working for greater speed and less accuracy or precision. (The executive function is explained further later on.) In the case of work underload, the individual might engage in conversation with co-workers, play the radio, or do something else while the jobs in the low-volume task pile up to a critical mass. When demand exceeds the coping zones in either direction, there is a sharp drop in performance that Hancock and Warm (1989) characterized as resembling the catastrophe function that is examined here.

Note that the possible coping strategies just mentioned constitute some degrees of freedom inherent in the task situation that the operator can juggle. I return to the principle of degrees of freedom later on in this chapter.

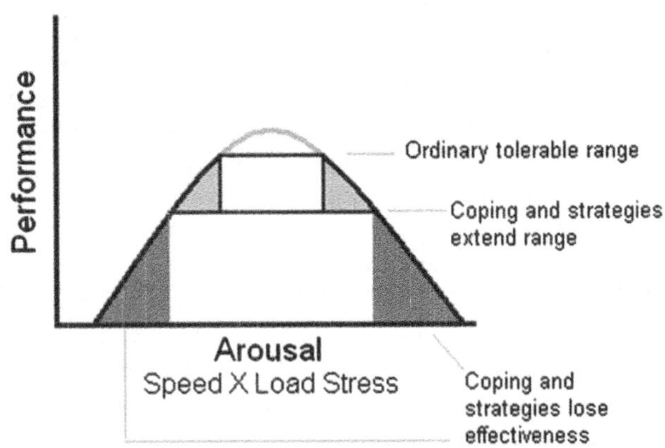

Fig. 2.2 The effect of arousal and coping strategies on performance based on the theory by Hancock and Warm (Reprinted from Guastello (2014, p. 202) with permission of Taylor and Francis)

The current consensus in the human factors community is that the measurement of cognitive workload is highly relative to the task environment; as an example, workload for air traffic controllers is closely tied to the number of aircraft trying to take off or land and weather conditions within a given time frame (Loft et al. 2007). In other words, workload cannot be calibrated in bits and bytes; not all bits and bytes are created equal psychologically. The measurement of the effects of workload can center on performance levels or error rates, subjective ratings, or physiological indicators such as ratings such as the P300 wave from an electroencephalograph (EEG) or arousal measured by the galvanic skin response (GSR), heart rate or breathing rate; for a review see (Funke et al. 2012). Subjective ratings are useful for comparing different configurations of a task and for their potential to catch differences in workload that would be buffered by the operators' adaptive responses and thus not appear in behavioral performance criteria. There is some concern, however, that the subjective ratings sometimes correspond with behavioral outcomes, and sometimes trend in different directions (Guastello et al. 2015b; Hancock 1996; Oron-Gilad et al. 2008; Yeh and Wickens 1988). Physiological measures capture signs of workload early in the perception-cognition-action process, and are now being explored for possible implementation in adaptive human-machine interfaces (Schmorrow and Stanney 2008). A comparison of different physiological metrics indicated that they do not always measure the same features of workload at the same time (Matthews et al. 2015).

The experimental study in the next chapter remains focused on the behavioral indicators of workload and fatigue for three reasons. First the behavioral measurements reflect the net results of cognitive and adaptive activities. Second, the discontinuities in performance are of primary concern theoretically. Third the intermediate cognitive or emotional processes are thought to be captured in the variability of performance, which is at least as important as differences between conditional means to the explanations afforded by the cusp catastrophe models and other NDS models.

2.1.3 Fatigue

Fatigue is the loss of work capacity over time. It is observed as either a decline in performance or a decline in the measurement of a central ability such as isometric strength (measured with a dynamometer) in a physical task. Cognitive fatigue studies, however, are mostly centered on performance, however, and the earliest examples date back over a century (Ackerman 2011). A classic and persistent finding, however, is the *work curve* shown in Fig. 2.3. Performance is relatively high and consistent for a while, then drops sharply. Variability in performance also increases during the period when performance is dropping.

Although fatigue can result from working under a high load level for too long, if the operator is working under too low a workload, switching to higher-demand task

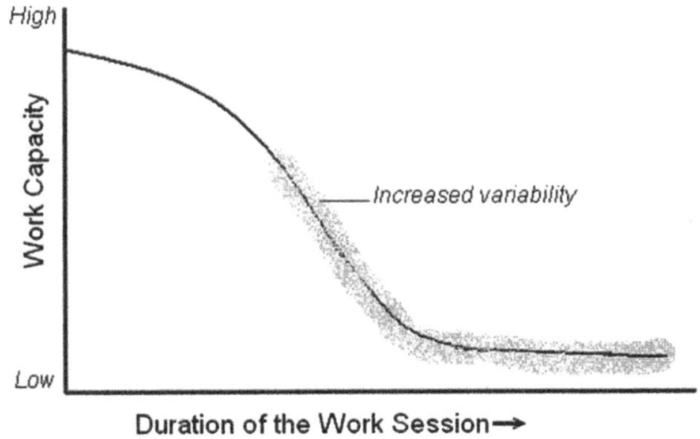

Fig. 2.3 The fatigue curve (Reprinted from Guastello (2014, p. 211) with permission of Taylor and Francis)

can relieve fatigue (Alves and Kelsey 2010; Lorist and Faber 2011). Switching tasks could be mentally costly, however, because task switching puts a demand on working memory to keep multiple task rules active simultaneously (Andreadis and Quinlan 2010; Lorist et al. 2000; Rubinstein et al. 2001).

Fatigue could result from total time working or from the time spent on a particular task. All other things being equal, the time spent on a particular task is more likely to produce a fatigue effect than total time working on a variety of tasks (Guastello et al. 2012b). Time on task can also produce a learning, practice, or momentum effect that produces an *improvement* in performance over time (Guastello and McGee 1987). It is also possible to observe rebound effects where performance drops, presumably as a result of fatigue, and improves again with no rest period in between (Guastello et al. 2013a).

The primary explanation for cognitive fatigue is that it results from prolonged demands on the executive function of working memory (Helton and Russell 2011, 2013, 2015; Logie 2011; Thomson et al. 2015). Performance decrements similar to the one shown in Fig. 2.3 have become a substantial concern in vigilance and other tasks that require sustained attention to a limited range of stimuli. Mindlessness (mind-wandering), and cognitive resource depletion have been studied as explanations for the performance decrement (Dillard et al. 2014; Warm et al. 2015). Mindlessness can result from the executive function playing a progressively smaller role in task performance while automatic processing takes over; it can be observed in the form of task-unrelated thoughts. Resource depletion can be alleviated somewhat by introducing rest periods (Ariga and Lleras 2011; Thomson et al. 2015). The mindlessness and resource depletion explanations are both consistent with the definition of fatigue as a reduction in work capacity and the cognitive deficits resulting more specifically from demand on the executive function of working memory.

Table 2.1 summaries the effects of the two basic divisions of working memory on performance decrements caused by taxing the maximum channel capacity and decrements produced by fatigue. The distinctions depicted in the table can be

Table 2.1 Working memory functions and CWLF[a]

	Working memory	
Inhibition, focus of attention, task shifting, and updating	**Executive functions**	**Fatigue Effect**
Math, verbal, spatial, episodic, psychomotor	**Workspace allocations**	**Workload and speed Effects**

[a]Reprinted from Guastello et al. (2014c, p. 306) with permission of the Society for Chaos Theory in Psychology & Life Sciences

somewhat misleading because the executive function is responsible for making the workspace allocations.

There is also a branch of fatigue research that is concerned with long times on tasks such as extended periods of motor vehicle driving. Fatigue in those situations is often conflated with disruptions of circadian rhythm or hours since the operator slept last. Because the present study involved short-term fatigue in a laboratory experiment, sleep-related sources of fatigue were not examined further here.

2.1.4 *Risk Taking and Stress*

Financial decisions are more often of the optimizing type where the decision maker is faced with several options and needs to invest available resources into the best choices. Most decisions, however, involve an element of uncertainty or risk. Using the economists' preferred definitions in Chap. 1, the experiment that follows involves risk, rather than uncertainty, because the participants were told what the odds of an outcome were determined to be (by someone not disclosed). Uncertainty, which involves *not knowing* what the odds of success or failure happen to be, is an issue addressed in a later chapter.

We can now merge the lines of thought from economics and human factors further. In the simple dichotomous signal detection task, the operator is watching stimuli and indicating the presence or absence of a target. The element of risk takes the form of the base rate of targets, which is usually not told to the operators in experiment, and is often unknown in the real world. Risk taking behavior is implicit in the two types of errors – misses and false alarms. It is well known that biases toward one type of error or the other are influenced by the costs associated with each type of error. The base rate of the target stimuli also affects the accuracy rate (Warm and Jerison 1984). In at least one experiment that measured time to respond to stimuli, fatigue had the effect of improving overall performance, but it did so by splitting the response time to make the two types of errors into increasing and decreasing directions (Hancock 2014; Parasuraman and Davies 1976). In cases like these, operators were becoming tired and missing stimuli altogether, which had the side effect of cutting down on false positives. It is also another type of example where time on task has positive and negative outcomes simultaneously.

In the type of financial decisions studied here, the operators are faced with multiple options and must choose the best one. They could make their choices by mentally computing the expected outcomes, or they could disengage their executive functions a bit by making their choices based on a subjective impression. Many cost-benefit decisions are actually based on subjective or *experiential* assessments of risk, according to Slovic and Peters (2006). There is a tendency for the decision maker to minimize the subjective risk or costs if the expected gains appear to be greater. This tendency in turn is magnified by stress induced by time pressure (Finucane et al. 2000; Fraser-Mackenzie and Dror 2011), a recent history of losses (Hunton et al. 2001), or sources unrelated to the decision environment such as intense cold (Porcelli and Delgado 2009). It remains to be seen (in the next chapter) how often stress promotes risk taking or risk aversion, and what individual differences in people predispose them to respond one way or another.

2.1.5 Cusp Catastrophe Models

Catastrophe theory describes and predicts sudden changes of events through use of seven elementary topological models. The cusp model is one of the simpler models in the series, and depicts changes between two stable states. For further background on the canonical cusp model, its role in the broader scope of nonlinear dynamics, its applications in applied psychology, and the analysis of cusp models in real data see Thom (1975) Zeeman (1977), Guastello (1995, 2013), Guastello and Gregson (2011) and Guastello and Liebovitch (2009).

The cusp surface is 3-dimensional and features a 2-dimensional manifold (unfolding). It describes two stable states of behavior (Fig. 2.4). Change between the two states is a function of two control parameters, *asymmetry* (a) and *bifurcation* (b). At low values of b, change is smooth, and at high values of b it is potentially discontinuous, depending on the values of a. At low values of a when b is high, changes occur around the lower mode and are relatively small in size. At middle values of a, changes occur between modes and are relatively large, assuming b is also large. At high values of a, changes occur around the upper mode and are again small.

The cusp response surface is the set of points where

$$\delta f(y)/\delta y = y^3 - by - a. \tag{2.1}$$

It can also be expressed as an implicit differential over time:

$$dy/dt = y^3 - by - a \tag{2.2}$$

Change in behavior is denoted by the path of a control point over time. The point begins on the upper sheet denoting behavior of one type, and is observed in that behavioral modality for a period of time. During that time its coordinates on a and

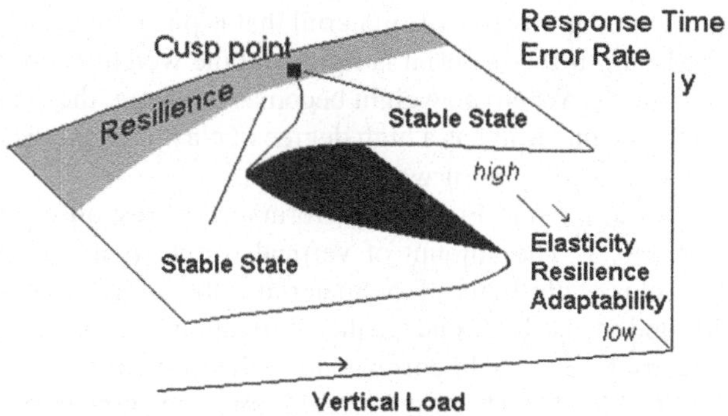

Fig. 2.4 Cusp catastrophe model for workload

b are changing when suddenly it reaches a fold line and drops to the lower value of the behavior, which is qualitatively different where it remains. Reversing direction, the point is observed in the lower mode until coordinates change to a critical pair of values, at which moment the point jumps back to the upper mode. There are two thresholds for behavior change, one ascending, and one descending. The phenomenon of *hysteresis* simultaneously refers to relatively frequent changes between the two behavioral states and the two different thresholds for change.

The shaded area of the surface is the region of inaccessibility in which very few points fall. Statistically, one would observe an antimode between the two stable states that would correspond to the shaded region of the surface.

The cusp and higher order catastrophe models contain a bifurcation set that appears in some drawings of the cusp in the general literature. The bifurcation set is essentially a 2-dimensional shadow of the unfolding of the surface. When viewed on the response surface itself, the cusp bifurcation set induces two diverging response gradients, which start at the stable states (attractors) and are joined at a *cusp point*. Behavior at the cusp point is ambiguous. The cusp point is known as the *point of degenerate singularity* and is the most unstable point on the surface. Analogous points exist in other catastrophe models as well.

The cusp model has a potential function also, which is the integral of the equation for the response surface. The potential function is not used here, but it is noteworthy that it is sometimes used in studies that involve self-organizing systems and phase shifts.

2.1.5.1 Buckling Model for Workload

The cusp model for cognitive workload invokes the concept of Euler buckling (Zeeman 1977), which was first introduced in a physical labor context some time ago (Guastello 1985). A piece of material that is subjected to sufficient amounts of stress in the form of repeated stretching will show a certain amount of deformity, or strain. Rigid materials will break, whereas flexible materials will rebound. The amount of permanent deformity induced by stress is the *stress–strain ratio*. Imagine a beam of relatively stiff material that is pin-jointed at both ends. Place a weight on the beam. If the material is rigid, and the weight is not supercritical, the beam will not buckle. When the weight becomes too large, the beam will snap. If, on the other hand, the material has a high degree of elasticity, increasing weight would cause the beam to waffle, but it would not snap.

In Eq. 2.2 and Fig. 2.4, performance or response time would be the dependent variable, y. The amount of vertical weight is the asymmetry (a) parameter. The modulus of elasticity of the material is the bifurcation factor (b), with low elasticity located at the high end of the bifurcation axis. Coping strategies, resilience, and anxiety levels would correspond to the bifurcation variable.

Workload has been measured in previous uses of the cusp model as a feature of the task that was experimentally manipulated or inherent in the task in some other way. Successful examples have included the peak memory span that a participant attempted to use in an episodic memory task (Guastello et al. 2012a), competitive versus noncompetitive incentive conditions in an pictorial memory task (Guastello et al. 2012b), task difficulty in a set of perceptual-motor tasks (Guastello et al. 2013a), and the speeding up or slowing down of stimulus rates in a vigilance task (Guastello et al. 2014b).

There was an attempt to evaluate experimental conditions where the participants worked alone or in pairs on the vigilance task, but this manipulation did not contribute to the load parameter in the cusp model. It did have an effect in static linear models, however, in that working in pairs did result in fewer errors on the vigilance task, more accomplished on the secondary task, but greater perceived demands for performance and for time pressure (Guastello et al. 2015b). Thus working in pairs did not produce any more or less of a change in performance in response to the other experimental manipulations, but it did affect absolute performance levels. Further research on dyads and teams in response to workload is much needed, but falls outside the scope of the present effort.

The construct of *elasticity* versus *rigidity* bears some resemblance to the construct of resilience that appears in other contexts. Several constructs of resilience have actually been applied to work systems (Hollnagel 2011; Hollnagel et al. 2006; Leonhardt et al. 2009; Woods and Wreathall 2008; Sheridan 2008) that employ the reasoning of complex dynamical systems (Guastello 2014). The particular principle of resilience versus rigidity for work systems that involves a system or person experiencing an increased level of workload and a stress–strain relationship that ensues (Woods and Wreathall 2008) is synonymous with "elasticity" in the present context. Pincus and Metten (2010) invoked a similar construct of resilience in a clinical context to describe conditions that promote functional and dysfunctional reactions to traumatic stress. In either type of example, rigidity buffers the stressor enough to maintain performance or apparent functionality, but too much stress applied to a rigid system results in sudden dysfunctionality. It is important to observe, however, that resilience might appear "better," but resilience by itself is not locally stable. Note its (alleged) location around the cusp point in Fig. 2.4. A resilient system is indeed very flexible but can be pushed into either a functional or dysfunctional stable state relatively easily. In any event, six psychosocial variables were studied as elasticity variables here in the context of cognitive workload: anxiety, frustration, emotional intelligence, conscientiousness, work ethic, and a cognitive style known as field independence.

Anxiety involves a modicum of arousal of the sympathetic nervous system. It can be a state, as when somebody experiences apprehension for a significant negative outcome. It can also be a trait, such that some individuals exhibit higher levels of arousal regularly. Trait anxiety can result from a circular relationship between further individual differences in the activity levels of the nervous system and stressful stimuli over many years (Eysenck 1997; Leary and Kowalski 1995). Anxiety can detract from performance by producing intrusive thoughts that hinder decision-making if it is triggered by a threatening cue (Ladoucer et al. 2009) or when arousal levels that are induced by the task are low (Vytal et al. 2012). Anxiety can also produce a positive effect on performance by heightening attentiveness to potentially threatening work conditions (Ein-Dor et al. 2010), and thus has potential as a bifurcation variable in some circumstances.

Anxiety showed a bifurcating impact on individual accident involvements in a manufacturing setting, such that people reporting higher levels of anxiety experienced notably more *or* fewer accidents than others, given the same range of hazard exposures (Guastello 2003; Guastello and Lynn 2014). It also worked as an elasticity variable in a memory task that was assessed with the buckling model in Fig. 2.4, in which the participants competed against other participants for extra class credits (Guastello et al. 2012b). It did not work as a bifurcation variable in some other workload studies, however, (Guastello et al. 2012a, 2013a, 2014b), although it did exhibit some simple linear relations with some indices of subjective workload (Guastello et al. 2015b). It now appears that anxiety becomes an active variable when people work together in teams or pairs (Naber et al. 2015).

Frustration, as it is used in the present context, is a subjective workload rating that is part of the NASA Task Load Index (TLX; Hart and Staveland 1988), which is widely used in human factors studies. It contains six ratings for mental demand, physical demand, temporal demand, performance demand, effort required to meet the performance goal, and frustration. The rating scales are usually given to research participants after performing a task and are often used to compare different task designs. Subjective ratings and their concordance with performance measures are examined in Chap. 4 for the financial decision making task.

Frustration reflects a distinct negative emotional reaction that might reflect a limit to the control and regulation functions defined by the other variables just described. Frustration in the context of the cusp models could be associated with negative performance or it could be an interim reaction prior to regrouping one's strategy for performing the task effectively. It acted as a bifurcation variable in a recent study involving a vigilance dual task (Guastello et al. 2014b).

Mayer and Salovey (1997) defined *emotional intelligence* (EI) as the ability "to perceive accurately, appraise, and express emotion; the ability to access and/or generate feelings when they facilitate thought; the ability to understand emotion and emotional knowledge; and the ability to regulate emotions to promote emotional and intellectual growth" (Mayer 2001, p. 10). There are currently several measurement models of EI, ranging from a more narrow focus on its cognitive aspects to broader definitions that emphasize its psychosocial aspects. The long-run correlations with work performance tend to run higher for the broader definitions (Joseph and Newman 2010). The measurement model developed by Schutte et al. (1998) was used in the present study because it captured the theme of *alexithymia,* which is the inability to interpret one's emotions and having no words to express one's emotions. There is a connection between high stress, emotional reactions, and the ability to detect those reactions and mitigate the situation effectively (Thompson 2010); failure to do so could result in bad decisions. According to Thompson, who also invoked a similar cusp model for stress and performance, low EI tends towards rigidity and high EI towards elasticity. The overall role of EI might be limited, however, to high stress jobs or jobs where a substantial amount of emotional labor is involved (Joseph and Newman 2010).

Writing from a different perspective that was framed around the construct of task engagement, (Matthews et al. 2010) made a good case for the importance of EI in conjunction with load, fatigue, and anxiety issues:

> Effects of stressors on performance operate within a larger self-regulative process ... The person's evaluation of their own mental functioning contributes to appraisals of stress and well-being, and may drive corrective coping efforts. For example, anxious individuals may apply compensatory effort to mitigate loss of processing efficiency resulting from worry ... Fatigued drivers take rest breaks or attempt to raise their own arousal ... Performance change must be understood in the wider context of the dynamic interactions between operator and task environment (p. 206).

One attempt to test EI as a bifurcation variable in the vigilance dual task did not work out as expected (Guastello et al. 2014b), although there were some linear relationships with performance pressure and perceived effort demands and some interactions with the experimental condition of working alone or in pairs (Guastello et al. 2015b). Persons scoring higher in EI reported greater performance pressure and greater demands for the effort needed to reach performance goals. Interaction effects were obtained for perceived temporal demands and effort demands such that the correlation between EI and demands was positive for those working in pairs and negative for those working alone. The role of EI was investigated again in the next chapter in which the participants in the experiment worked alone, and load was manipulated by the contents of the stimuli as well as by adjusting work speed.

Conscientiousness is a personality trait whereby someone with a high score would be attentive to details in their work and daily life, adherent to rules, exert optimal effort for accomplishing the task, and exhibit self-control rather than impulsiveness (Cattell et al. 1970; McCrae and Costa 1985). Conscientiousness predicts performance in a wide range of jobs although the relationships are generally small (Meyer et al. 2009). According to MacLean and Arnell (2010), the conscientious person's ability to focus attention could be intrinsic to maintaining rigidity of performance. Conscientiousness could act as a buffer against workload, although with the same liabilities as bifurcation variables related to rigidity. One previous attempt to test conscientiousness as a bifurcation variable in the vigilance task did not work out as expected, however (Guastello et al. 2014b), although it did show a linear correlation with miss errors and perceived temporal demands (Guastello et al. 2015b).

Conscientiousness is well recognized as one of the factors of the five factor model (FFM) of personality. There is growing evidence, however, that narrower definitions of personality traits have a stronger connection to behavior than their FFM parent constructs (Dudley et al. 2006; Guastello et al. 2014a; Szymura 2010; Guastello et al. 2015b). In the case of the vigilance dual task, separating FFM conscientiousness into a narrow construct of conscientiousness and impulsivity resulted in both variables correlating with perceived temporal demands in opposite directions. Highly controlled individuals perceived the dual task as having greater time pressure than did other participants, but those scoring higher on the narrower consciousness construct perceived less temporal demand than other participants. In light of these complexities, the conscientiousness construct was operationalized as two constructs in this study.

The *Protestant Work Ethic* (PWE) is a set of beliefs about work that emphasizes independent action, free will, and an obligation to work (Buchholz 1977; Furnham 1990; Stillman et al. 2010). A person who endorses the work ethic would be likely to maintain effort on boring or tedious tasks (Greenberg 1977). PWE was a dominant work value in the US up until the late 1970s. It still exists in Western society, with independence and beliefs about free will being its most salient features. PWE is expected to have the same relationship to performance differences as conscientiousness under conditions of challenging workload. Curiously, PWE was found to have a positive linear correlation with a static measure of miss errors (Guastello et al. 2015b), which was the opposite of what was expected and not readily explicable. The role of PWE was investigated again in the present study.

Field dependence versus *independence* is the ability to identify a target in a complex visual field and separate it from the background material. The construct is actually classified as a *cognitive style*, which has attributes of an ability and a personality characteristic (Kozhenikov et al. 2014). Cognitive styles represent the way people use their abilities rather than particular levels of the abilities. Field independent people are more apt to see the target separated from its background and context, whereas field dependent people are more apt to respond to background elements at the possible exclusion of elements that could be salient targets for others. The primary measurement of field independence or dependence is the Group Embedded Figures Test (GEFT; Witkin et al. 1971). It has surfaced as a bifurcation variable in cognitive workload associated with solving chemistry problems (Stamovlasis 2006, 2011; Stamovlasis and Tsaparlis 2012), under the premise that field-independent people make better use of their working memory capacities (Pascual-Leone 1970). Of further interest, Mykytyn (1989) compared scores on GEFT for entry-level and expert financial analysts, with the result that the experts were more field independent. Thus it seemed worthwhile to pursue this effect further in the context of the present study; to our knowledge, Mykytyn's study was the only connection between GEFT and financial decision making ever reported.

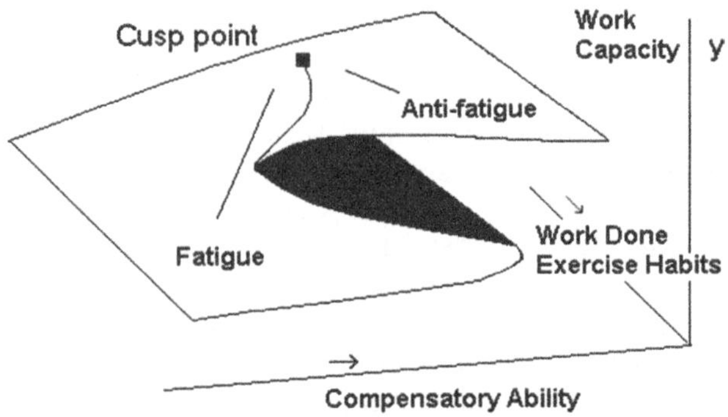

Fig. 2.5 Cusp catastrophe model for fatigue

2.1.5.2 Fatigue

Fatigue, which is defined as the loss of work capacity, is typically observed as a *work curve* that plots performance over time; there is a sharp drop in performance when fatigue sets in that is also coupled with a higher level of performance variability over time as fatigue sets in. Not everyone experiences a decline as result of the same expenditures, however. Some show an increase in physical strength akin to "just getting warmed up," while others show stably high or lower performance levels for the duration of the work period. Learning, practice, and automaticity effects, which also serve to move performance upward rather than downward, were discussed in an earlier section of this article.

Ioteyko (1920) introduced a cubic polynomial function to account for the full range of possible work curves, which essentially comprised the cusp catastrophe model for fatigue (Guastello and McGee 1987; Fig. 2.5). Work capacity is the dependent measure that displays two stable states. Change in capacity is implied by change in performance. The total quantity of work done would be the main contributor to the bifurcation parameter: If the individual did not accomplish much in a fixed amount of time, there would be comparably little drain on work capacity. Those who accomplished more could exhibit either positive or negative changes in work capacity.

The asymmetry parameter would be a compensatory strength measure. For instance, in Guastello and McGee (1987), laborers displayed differences in arm strength as a result of about 2 h worth of standard mill labor tasks, which primarily demanded arm strength. Leg strength, however, acted as a compensation factor for arm strength; those with greater leg strength experienced less fatigue in their arms.

The strategy for choosing abilities to test in the first cognitive fatigue models in our series was to sample broadly from cognitive domains. For instance, ability in speeded arithmetic worked as a compensatory ability in an episodic memory task (Guastello et al. 2012a), peak episodic memory span worked for a pictorial memory task (Guastello et al. 2012b); spelling worked for only one out of seven perceptual-motor tasks (Guastello et al. 2013a) and for none of the previously mentioned tasks. For the vigilance task, the effective ability variable was an experimental condition of speeding up or slowing down; the changing work speed was not an ability per se, but interpreted as a training regimen for whatever abilities happened to be involved (Guastello et al. 2014b). The current strategy for investigating abilities has shifted to some extent to focus on variables from the fluid intelligence domain because the current thinking in cognitive psychology is that working memory is part of fluid intelligence, and the executive function is supervenient to the more basic abilities and workspace areas and functions (Conway et al. 2005; Kane et al. 2005; Nusbaum and Silvia 2011; Oberauer and Kleigel 2006).

The compensatory abilities that were investigated in the present study were basic arithmetic and spelling again, an anagram test, and field dependence versus independence. Arguably, arithmetic ability is probably more direct than indirect in the present context.

Anagram tests are cognitive measures of creative thinking (Barron 1955; Lehman and Gavurin 1975; Mendelsohn and Griswold 1964) and a part of fluid intelligence (Hakstian and Cattell 1978; Nusbaum and Silvia 2011). An anagram is a set of letters of the alphabet that do not make a word in the order in which they are presented, but the participant must re-order the letters to make a word. It should be noted that the task in the present experiment involves a convergent optimizing task, which favors one best answer, rather than a divergent task that requires many possible original answers.

2.1.5.3 Degrees of Freedom

Catastrophe models, phase shifts and self-organizing dynamics are closely related (Gilmore 1981; Guastello 2005; Haken 1988). Self-organizing dynamics commonly result from interactions, information flows or communications among the subsystems. The concept of degrees of freedom, as implemented by Turvey (1990) in conjunction with physical movements, provides further explanation of the role of coping or flexibility variables in cognitive workload dynamics. The concept also explains to some extent why the upper limits to cognitive channel capacity can be variable.

In any particular complex movement, each limb of the body is capable of moving in a limited number of ways, and the movements made by one limb restrict or facilitate movement by other limbs. The notion of internally connected nodes of movement is substantially more efficient, and simpler, than assuming that all elements of movement are controlled by a central executive function (Turvey 1990). When a movement is in its earliest stages of being learned, several neuromotor combinations are explored by the individual; but once learning sets in, the movement combinations gravitate towards the conservation of degrees of freedom, which makes the action more efficient. The improved efficiency is in turn reflected in less variability in performance (Friston 2010; Hong 2010). The learning process is actually a self-organization dynamic, such that a system adopts a structure that requires less entropy to carry out its function. Some variability in the movement still persists in healthy systems, however, which facilitates new affordances or variations in stimuli from the environment or the definition of new goals originated by the individual (Abbott et al. 2005; Hristovski et al. 2006, 2011; Mayer-Kress et al. 2009; Stergiou et al. 2006). The net result is a paradox in which consistency of performance is one goal, but maintaining variability is another (Guastello et al. 2013b, 2014c). Sufficiently large changes in goals or demands produce phase shifts in the motor movements, which are observed as discontinuous changes in the sense of catastrophe models.

Cognitive behaviors are thought to operate on more or less the same principle with regard to the early and later stages of schematic development, the role of executive functions and the principle of conserving degrees of freedom (Hollis et al. 2009). For a given type of task, the executive function could play a prominent role during skill acquisition and the earlier stages of mastery, but could relinquish its involvement as the execution becomes more automatic. Because cognition is often tied to action, the span of relevant degrees of freedom includes the whole perception-action sequence in the sense of Gibson's (1979) ecological perspective.

According to Hong (2010), the increased variability in performance that sets in during fatigue is a sign of an impending phase shift in one of two types. In one scenario, entropy could drop to zero, meaning that the person stops performing the task. In the other, a cognitive reorganization strategy is employed that gives the appearance of a "second wind." Voluntary task switching could be considered an example of either type of response to fatigue, but second-wind or rebound effects have been observed independently of task switching or rest periods (Guastello et al. 2013a).

Finally, to close the proverbial loop, anxiety, conscientiousness and EI were tested as asymmetry variables in the fatigue model for financial decision making. This was done mostly to address the possibility that non-cognitive variables could affect the way cognitive abilities are used or managed under conditions of fatigue. Also, risk taking has a substantial emotional component to it, "calculated risks" notwithstanding. Thus there was a possibility that anxiety, conscientiousness and EI could affect the fatigue model for risk taking, even if it did not do so for optimizing.

References

Abbott, A., Button, C., Pepping, G.-J., & Collins, D. (2005). Unnatural selection: Talent identification and development in sport. *Nonlinear Dynamics, Psychology, and Life Sciences, 9*, 61–88.

Ackerman, P. L. (Ed.). (2011). *Cognitive fatigue*. Washington, DC: American Psychological Association.

Alves, E. E., & Kelsey, C. M. (2010). Combating vigilance decrement in a single-operator radar platform. *Ergonomics in Design, 18*(2), 6–9.

Andreadis, N., & Quinlan, P. T. (2010). Task switching under predictable and unpredictable circumstances. *Attention, Perception, and Psychophysics, 72*, 1776–1790.

Ariga, A., & Lleras, A. (2011). Brief and rare mental "breaks" keep you focused: Deactivation and reactivation of task goals preempt vigilance decrements. *Cognition, 118*, 439–443.

Baddeley, A. (2003). Working memory: Looking back and looking forward. *Nature Reviews Neuroscience, 4*, 829–839.

Barron, F. (1955). The disposition toward originality. *The Journal of Abnormal and Social Psychology, 51*, 478–485.

Buchholz, R. A. (1977). The belief structure of managers relative to work concepts measured by a factor analytic model. *Personnel Psychology, 30*, 567–587.

Cattell, R. B., Eber, H. W., & Tatsuoka, M. M. (1970). *Handbook for the sixteen personality factor questionnaire*. Champaign: Institute for Personality and Ability Testing.

Conrad, R. (1951). Speed and load stress in a sensorimotor skill. *British Journal of Industrial Medicine, 8*, 1–7.

Conway, A. R. A., Kane, M. J., Bunting, M. F., Hambrick, D. Z., & Engle, R. W. (2005). Working memory span tasks: A methodological review and user's guide. *Psychonomic Bulletin & Review, 12*, 769–786.

Dillard, M. B., Warm, J. S., Funke, G. J., Funke, M. E., Finomore, V. S., Matthews, G., Shaw, T. H., & Parasuraman, R. (2014). The sustained attention to response task (SART) does not promote mindlessness during vigilance performance. *Human Factors, 56*, 1364–1379.

Dudley, N. M., Orvis, K. A., Lebiecki, J. E., & Cortina, J. M. (2006). A meta-analytic investigation of conscientiousness in the prediction of job performance: Examining the intercorrelations and the incremental validity of narrow traits. *Journal of Applied Psychology, 91*, 40–57.

Ein-Dor, T., Mikulincer, M., Doron, G., & Shaver, P. R. (2010). The attachment paradox: How can so many of us (the insecure ones) have no adaptive advantages. *Perspectives on Psychological Science, 5*, 123–141.

Eysenck, M. W. (1997). *Anxiety and cognition: A unified theory*. New York: Psychology Press/ Taylor & Francis.

Finucane, M. L., Alhakami, A., Slovic, P., & Johnson, S. M. (2000). The affect heuristic in judgments of risks and benefits. *Journal of Behavioral Decision Making, 13*, 1–17.

Fraser-Mackenzie, P. A. F., & Dror, I. E. (2011). Dynamic reasoning and time pressure: Transition from analytical operations to experiential responses. *Theory and Decision, 71*, 211–225.

Friston, K. (2010). The free-energy principle: A unified brain theory? *Nature Reviews Neuroscience, 11*(2), 127–138.

Funke, G. J., Knott, B. A., Salas, E., Pavlas, D., & Strang, A. J. (2012). Conceptualization and measurement of team workload: A critical need. *Human Factors, 54*, 36–51.

Furnham, A. (1990). A content, correlational, and factor analytic study of seven questionnaire measures of the Protestant work ethic. *Human Relations, 43*, 383–399.

Gibson, J. J. (1979). *The ecological approach to visual perception*. Boston: Houghton Mifflin.

Gilmore, R. (1981). *Catastrophe theory for scientists and engineers*. New York: Wiley.

Greenberg, J. (1977). The Protestant work ethic and reactions to negative performance evaluations on a laboratory task. *Journal of Applied Psychology, 62*, 682–690.

Guastello, S. J. (1985). Euler buckling in a wheelbarrow obstacle course: A catastrophe with complex lag. *Behavioral Science, 30*, 204–212.

Guastello, S. J. (1995). *Chaos, catastrophe, and human affairs: Applications of nonlinear dynamics to work, organizations, and social evolution*. Hillsdale: Lawrence Erlbaum Associates.

Guastello, S. J. (2003). Nonlinear dynamics, complex systems, and occupational accidents. *Human Factors and Ergonomics in Manufacturing & Service Industries, 13*, 293–304.

Guastello, S. J. (2005). Statistical distributions in self-organizing phenomena: What conclusions should be drawn? *Nonlinear Dynamics, Psychology, and Life Sciences, 9*, 463–478.

Guastello, S. J. (2013). Catastrophe theory and its applications to I/O psychology. In J. M. Cortina & R. Landis (Eds.), *Frontiers of methodology in organizational research* (pp. 29–62). New York: Routledge.

Guastello, S. J. (2014). *Human factors engineering and ergonomics: A systems approach* (2nd ed.). Boca Raton: CRC Press.

Guastello, S. J., & Gregson, R. A. M. (Eds.). (2011). *Nonlinear dynamical systems analysis for the behavioral sciences using real data*. Boca Raton: CRC Press.

Guastello, S. J., & Liebovitch, L. S. (2009). Introduction to nonlinear dynamics and complexity. In S. J. Guastello, M. Koopmans, & D. Pincus (Eds.), *Chaos and complexity in psychology: Theory of nonlinear dynamical systems* (pp. 1–40). New York: Cambridge University Press.

Guastello, S. J., & Lynn, M. (2014). Catastrophe model of the accident process, safety climate, and anxiety. *Nonlinear Dynamics, Psychology, and Life Sciences, 18*, 177–198.

Guastello, S. J., & McGee, D. W. (1987). Mathematical modeling of fatigue in physically demanding jobs. *Journal of Mathematical Psychology, 31*, 248–269.

Guastello, S. J., Boeh, H., Shumaker, C., & Schimmels, M. (2012a). Catastrophe models for cognitive workload and fatigue. *Theoretical Issues in Ergonomics Science, 13*, 586–602.

Guastello, S. J., Boeh, H., Schimmels, M., Gorin, H., Huschen, S., Davis, E., Peters, N. E., Fabisch, M., & Poston, K. (2012b). Cusp catastrophe models for cognitive workload and fatigue in a verbally-cued pictorial memory task. *Human Factors, 54*, 811–825.

Guastello, S. J., Boeh, H., Gorin, H., Huschen, S., Peters, N. E., Fabisch, M., & Poston, K. (2013a). Cusp catastrophe models for cognitive workload and fatigue: A comparison of seven task types. *Nonlinear Dynamics, Psychology, and Life Sciences, 17*, 23–47.

Guastello, S. J., Gorin, H., Huschen, S., Peters, N. E., Fabisch, M., Poston, K., & Weinberger, K. (2013b). The minimum entropy principle and task performance. *Nonlinear Dynamics, Psychology, and Life Sciences, 17*, 405–424.

Guastello, A. D., Guastello, S. J., & Guastello, D. D. (2014a). Personality trait theory and multitasking performance: Implications for ergonomic design. *Theoretical Issues in Ergonomics Science, 15*, 432–450. doi:10.1080/1463922X.2012.762063.

Guastello, S. J., Malon, M., Timm, P., Weinberger, K., Gorin, H., Fabisch, M., & Poston, K. (2014b). Catastrophe models for cognitive workload and fatigue in a vigilance dual-task. *Human Factors, 56*, 737–751.

Guastello, S. J., Reiter, K., Shircel, A., Timm, P., Malon, M., & Fabisch, M. (2014c). The performance-variability paradox, financial decision making, and the curious case of negative Hurst exponents. *Nonlinear Dynamics, Psychology, and Life Sciences, 18*, 297–328.

Guastello, S. J., Reiter, K., Malon, M., Timm, P., Shircel, A., & Shaline, J. (2015a). Catastrophe models for cognitive workload and fatigue in N-back tasks. *Nonlinear Dynamics, Psychology, and Life Sciences, 19*, 173–200.

Guastello, S. J., Shircel, A., Malon, M., & Timm, P. (2015b). Individual differences in the experience of cognitive workload. *Theoretical Issues in Ergonomics Science, 16*, 20–52.

Haken, H. (1988). *Information and self-organization: A macroscopic approach to complex systems*. New York: Springer.

Hakstian, A. R., & Cattell, R. B. (1978). Higher-stratum ability structures on a basis of twenty primary abilities. *Journal of Educational Psychology, 70*, 657–669.

Hancock, P. A. (1996). Effects of control order, augmented feedback, input device and practice on tracking performance and perceived workload. *Ergonomics, 39*, 1146–1162.

Hancock, P. A. (2013). In search of vigilance: The problem of iatrogenically created psychological phenomena. *American Psychologist, 68*, 97–109.

Hancock, P. A. (2014). Finding vigilance through complex explanations for complex phenomena. *American Psychologist, 69*, 86–88.

Hancock, P. A., & Desmond, P. A. (Eds.). (2001). *Stress, workload, and fatigue*. Mahwah: Lawrence Erlbaum Associates.

Hancock, P. A., & Warm, J. S. (1989). A dynamic model of stress and sustained attention. *Human Factors, 31*, 519–537.

Hart, S. G., & Staveland, L. E. (1988). Development of the NASA task load index (TLX): Results of experimental and theoretical research. In P. A. Hancock & N. Meshkati (Eds.), *Human workload* (pp. 138–183). Amsterdam: North-Holland.

Helton, W. S., & Russell, P. N. (2011). Working memory load and the vigilance decrement. *Experimental Brain Research, 212*, 429–437.

Helton, W. S., & Russell, P. N. (2013). Visuospatial and verbal working memory load: Effects on visuospatial vigilance. *Experimental Brain Research, 224*, 429–436.

Helton, W. S., & Russell, P. N. (2015). Rest is best: The role of rest and task interruptions on vigilance. *Cognition, 134*, 165–173.
Hollis, G., Kloos, H., & Van Orden, G. C. (2009). Origins of order in cognitive activity. In S. J. Guastello, M. Koopmans, & D. Pincus (Eds.), *Chaos and complexity in psychology: The theory of nonlinear dynamical systems* (pp. 206–242). New York: Cambridge University Press.
Hollnagel, E. (2011). The score of resilience engineering. In E. Hollnagel, J. Paries, D. D. Woods, & J. Wreathall (Eds.), *Resilience engineering in practice: A guidebook* (pp. xxix–xxxix). Burlington: Ashgate.
Hollnagel, E., Woods, D. D., & Leveson, N. (Eds.). (2006). *Resilience engineering*. Burlington: Ashgate.
Holmes, T. H., & Rahe, R. H. (1967). The social readjustment rating scale. *Journal of Psychosomatic Research, 11*, 213–218.
Hong, S. L. (2010). The entropy conservation principle: Applications in ergonomics and human factors. *Nonlinear Dynamics, Psychology, and Life Sciences, 14*, 291–315.
Hristovski, R., Davids, K., & Araujo, D. (2006). Affordance-controlled bifurcations of action patterns in martial arts. *Nonlinear Dynamics, Psychology, and Life Sciences, 10*, 409–444.
Hristovski, R., Davids, K., Araujo, D., & Passos, P. (2011). Constraints-induced emergence of functional novelty in complex neurobiological systems: A basis for creativity in sport. *Nonlinear Dynamics, Psychology, and Life Sciences, 15*, 175–206.
Hunton, J. E., McEwen, R. A., & Bhattacharjee, S. (2001). Toward an understanding of the risk choice behavior of professional financial analysts. *The Journal of Psychology and Financial Markets, 2*, 182–189.
Ioteyko, J. (1920). *La fatigue [Fatigue]* (2nd ed.). Paris: Flammarion.
Joseph, D. L., & Newman, D. A. (2010). Emotional intelligence: An integrative meta-analysis and cascading model. *Journal of Applied Psychology, 95*, 54–78.
Kane, M. J., & Engle, R. W. (2002). The role of prefrontal cortex in working-memory capacity, executive attention, and general fluid intelligence: An individual-differences perspective. *Psychonomic Bulletin & Review, 9*, 617–671.
Kane, M. J., Hambrick, D. Z., & Conway, A. R. A. (2005). Working memory capacity and fluid intelligence are strongly related constructs: Comment on Ackerman, Beier, and Boyle (2005). *Psychological Bulletin, 131*, 66–71.
Kantowitz, B., & Sorkin, D. (1983). *Human factors: Understanding people-system relationships*. New York: Wiley.
Kozhenikov, M., Evans, C., & Kosslyn, S. M. (2014). Cognitive style as environmentally sensitive individual differences in cognition: A modern synthesis and applications in education, business, and management. *Psychological Science in the Public Interest, 15*, 1–33.
Ladoucer, C. D., Silk, J. S., Dahl, R. E., Ostapenko, L., Kronhaus, D. M., & Phillips, M. L. (2009). Fearful faces influence attentional control processes in anxious youth and adults. *Emotion, 9*, 855–864.
Leary, M. R., & Kowalski, R. M. (1995). *Social anxiety*. New York: Guilford Press.
Lehman, H. H., & Gavurin, E. I. (1975). Relationship of anagram solving to measures of divergent-production and letter rearrangement ability. *Journal of General Psychology, 92*, 231–236.
Leonhardt, J., Macchi, L., Hollnagel, E., & Kirwan, B. (2009). *A white paper on resilience engineering for ATM*. Eurocontrol. Retrieved March 9, 2011, from http://www.eurocontrol.int/esp/gallery/content/public/library
Loft, S., Sanderson, P., Neal, A., & Mooij, M. (2007). Modeling and predicting mental workload in en route air traffic control: Critical review and broader implications. *Human Factors, 49*, 376–399.
Logie, R. H. (2011). The functional organization and capacity limits of working memory. *Current Directions in Psychological Science, 20*, 240–245.

Lorist, M. M., & Faber, L. G. (2011). Consideration of the influence of mental fatigue on controlled and automatic cognitive processes. In P. Ackerman (Ed.), *Cognitive fatigue* (pp. 105–126). Washington, DC: American Psychological Association.

Lorist, M. M., Klein, M., Nieuwenhaus, S., De Jong, R., Mulder, G., & Meijman, T. F. (2000). Mental fatigue and task control: Planning and preparation. *Psychophysiology, 37*, 614–625.

MacLean, M. H., & Arnell, K. M. (2010). Personality predicts temporal attention costs in the attentional blink paradigm. *Psychonomic Bulletin & Review, 17*, 556–562.

Matthews, G., Warm, J. S., Reinerman, L. E., Lengheim, L. K., & Saxby, D. J. (2010). Task engagement, attention, and executive control. In A. Gruszka, G. Matthews, & B. Szymura (Eds.), *Handbook of individual differences in cognition* (pp. 205–230). New York: Springer.

Matthews, G., Desmond, P. A., Neubauer, C., & Hancock, P. A. (Eds.). (2012). *The handbook of operator fatigue*. Burlington: Ashgate.

Matthews, G., Reinerman-Jones, L. E., Barber, D. J., & Abich, J., IV. (2015). The psychometrics of mental workload: Multiples measures are sensitive but divergent. *Human Factors, 57*, 125–143.

Mayer, J. D. (2001). A field guide to emotional intelligence. In J. Ciarrochi, J. P. Forgas, & J. D. Mayer (Eds.), *Emotional intelligence in everyday life: A scientific inquiry* (pp. 3–24). Philadelphia: Taylor & Francis.

Mayer, J. D., & Salovey, P. (1997). What is emotional intelligence? In P. Salovey & D. Sluyter (Eds.), *Emotional development and emotional intelligence: Educational implications* (pp. 3–34). New York: Basic Books.

Mayer-Kress, G., Newell, K. M., & Liu, Y.-T. (2009). Nonlinear dynamics of motor learning. *Nonlinear Dynamics, Psychology, and Life Sciences, 13*, 3–26.

McCrae, R. R., & Costa, P. T., Jr. (1985). Updating Norman's "adequate taxonomy:" Intelligence and personality dimensions in natural language questionnaires. *Journal of Personality and Social Psychology, 49*, 710–721.

Mendelsohn, G. A., & Griswold, B. B. (1964). Differential use of incidental stimuli in problem solving as a function of creativity. *The Journal of Abnormal and Social Psychology, 68*, 431–436.

Meyer, R. D., Dalal, R. S., & Bonaccio, S. (2009). A meta-analytic investigation into the moderating effects of situational strength on the conscientiousness-performance relationship. *Journal of Organizational Behavior, 30*, 1077–1102.

Mykytyn, P. P., Jr. (1989). Group embedded figures test (GEFT): Individual differences, performance, and learning effects. *Educational and Psychological Measurement, 49*, 951–959.

Naber, A. M., McDonald, J. N., Asenuga, O. A., & Arthur, W., Jr. (2015). Team members' interaction anxiety and team training effectiveness: A catastrophic relationship? *Human Factors, 57*, 163–176.

Nusbaum, E. C., & Silvia, P. J. (2011). Are intelligence and creativity really so different? Fluid intelligence, executive processes, and strategy use in divergent thinking. *Intelligence, 39*, 36–45.

Oberauer, K., & Kleigel, R. (2006). A formal model of capacity limits in working memory. *Journal of Memory and Language, 55*, 601–626.

Oron-Gilad, T., Szalma, J. L., Stafford, S. C., & Hancock, P. A. (2008). The workload and performance relationship in the real world: A study of police officers in a field shooting exercise. *International Journal of Occupational Safety and Ergonomics, 14*, 119–131.

Parasuraman, R., & Davies, D. R. (1976). Decision theory analysis of response latencies in vigilance. *Journal of Experimental Psychology: Human Perception and Performance, 2*, 578–590.

Pascual-Leone, J. (1970). A mathematical model for the transition rule in Piaget's developmental stages. *Acta Psychologica, 32*, 301–345.

Pincus, D., & Metten, A. (2010). Nonlinear dynamics in biopsychosocial resilience. *Nonlinear Dynamics, Psychology, and Life Sciences, 14*, 353–380.

Porcelli, A. J., & Delgado, M. R. (2009). Acute stress modulates risk taking in financial decisions. *Psychological Science, 20*, 278–283.

Quick, J. C., & Quick, J. D. (1984). *Organizational stress and preventive management*. New York: McGraw-Hill.

Rubinstein, J. S., Meyer, D. E., & Evans, J. E. (2001). Executive control of cognitive processes in task switching. *Journal of Experimental Psychology: Human Perception and Performance, 27*, 763–797.

Schmorrow, D. D., & Stanney, K. M. (2008). *Augmented cognition: A practitioner's guide*. Santa Monica: Human Factors and Ergonomics Society.

Schutte, N. S., Malouf, J. M., Hall, L. E., Haggerty, D. J., Cooper, J. T., Golden, C. J., & Dornheim, L. (1998). Development and validation of a measure of emotional intelligence. *Personality and Individual Differences, 25*, 167–177.

Selye, H. (1976). *The stress of life* (2nd ed.). New York: McGraw-Hill.

Sheridan, T. B. (2008). Risk, human error, and system resilience: Fundamental ideas. *Human Factors, 50*, 418–426.

Slovic, P., & Peters, E. (2006). Risk perception and affect. *Current Directions in Psychological Science, 15*, 322–325.

Stamovlasis, D. (2006). The nonlinear dynamical hypothesis in science education problem solving: A catastrophe theory approach. *Nonlinear Dynamics, Psychology and Life Science, 10*, 37–70.

Stamovlasis, D. (2011). Nonlinear dynamics and neo-Piagetian theories in problem solving: Perspectives on a new epistemology and theory development. *Nonlinear Dynamics, Psychology and Life Science, 15*, 145–173.

Stamovlasis, D., & Tsaparlis, G. (2012). Applying catastrophe theory to an information-processing model of problem solving in science education. *Science Education, 96*, 392–410.

Stergiou, N., Harbourne, R. T., & Cavanaugh, J. T. (2006). Optimal movement variability: A new theoretical perspective for neurologic physical therapy. *Journal of Neurologic Physical Therapy, 30*, 120–129.

Stillman, T. F., Baumeister, R. F., Vohs, K. D., Lambert, N. M., Fincham, F. D., & Brewer, L. E. (2010). Personal philosophy and personnel achievement: Belief in free will predicts better job performance. *Social Psychological and Personality Science, 1*, 43–50.

Szymura, B. (2010). Individual differences in resource allocation policy. In A. Gruszka, G. Matthews, & B. Szymura (Eds.), *Handbook of individual differences in cognition: Attention, memory, and executive control* (pp. 231–246). New York: Springer.

Thom, R. (1975). *Structural stability and morphogenesis*. New York: Addison-Wesley.

Thompson, H. L. (2010). *The stress effect: Why smart leaders make dumb decisions – and what to do about it*. San Francisco: Jossey-Bass.

Thomson, D. R., Besnder, D., & Smilek, D. (2015). A resource-control account of sustained attention: Evidence from mind-wandering and vigilance paradigms. *Perspectives on Psychological Science, 10*, 82–96.

Turvey, M. T. (1990). Coordination. *American Psychologist, 45*, 938–953.

Vytal, K., Cornwell, B., Arkin, N., & Grillon, C. (2012). Describing the interplay between anxiety and cognition: From impaired performance under low cognitive load to reduced anxiety under high load. *Psychophysiology, 49*, 842–852.

Warm, J. S., & Jerison, H. J. (1984). The psychophysics of vigilance. In J. S. Warm (Ed.), *Sustained attention in human performance* (pp. 15–57). New York: Wiley.

Warm, J. S., Finomore, V. S., Vidulich, M. A., & Funke, M. E. (2015). Vigilance: A perceptual challenge. In R. R. Hoffman, P. A. Hancock, J. L. Szalma, & R. Parasuraman (Eds.), *Handbook of applied perception*. New York: Cambridge University Press.

Wickens, C. D. (2002). Multiple resources and performance prediction. *Theoretical Issues in Ergonomics Science, 3*, 159–177.

Wickens, C. D. (2008). Multiple resources and mental workload. *Human Factors, 50*, 449–455.

Witkin, H. A., Oltman, P. K., Raskin, E., & Karp, S. A. (1971). *A manual for the embedded figures test*. Palo Alto: Consulting Psychologists Press.

Woods, D. D., & Wreathall, J. (2008). Stress–strain plots as a basis for assessing system resilience. In E. Hollnagel, C. P. Nemeth, & S. W. A. Dekker (Eds.), *Resilience engineering: Remaining sensitive to the possibility of failure* (pp. 143–158). Aldershot: Ashgate.

Yeh, Y. Y., & Wickens, C. D. (1988). Association of performance and subjective measures of workload. *Human Factors, 30*, 111–120.

Yerkes, R. M., & Dodson, J. D. (1908). The relationship of strength of stimulus to rapidity of habit formation. *Journal of Comparative Neurology and Psychology, 18*, 459–482.

Zeeman, E. C. (1977). *Catastrophe theory: Selected papers, 1972–1977*. Reading: Addison-Wesley.

Zwerling, C., Daltroy, L. H., Fine, L. J., Johnston, J. J., Melius, J., & Silverstein, B. A. (1997). Design and conduct of occupational injury intervention studies: A review of evaluation strategies. *American Journal of Industrial Medicine, 32*, 164–179.

Chapter 3
Experimental Analysis of Cusp Models

Stephen J. Guastello, Anton Shircel, Matthew Malon, Paul Timm, Kelsey Gonring, and Katherine Reiter

Abstract This chapter presents an empirical assessment of the cusp catastrophe models for cognitive workload and fatigue as outlined in the previous chapter. Participants were 299 undergraduates who completed a series of psychological tests and measurements, which were followed by a financial decision making task that escalated in workload. The task required the participants to work in one of three speed conditions. Results supported both cusp models for both optimizing and risk taking criteria as evidenced by a superior degree of fit compared to the alternative linear models. For workload, conscientiousness and self-control as were the elasticity-rigidity (bifurcation) factors in optimizing, and field dependence and work ethic were elasticity variables in risk tasking; speed and decision complexity were the asymmetry variables. For fatigue, work completed and work speed were the bifurcation factors, as hypothesized, for both optimizing and risk taking; field independence was the asymmetry variable for both dependent measures, and performance on an anagram test was another compensatory ability that inhibited risk taking.

3.1 Hypotheses

In the experiment that follows, the participants evaluated sets of investment options and chose the one that they thought provided the best expected outcomes. The sets of options were organized into six blocks. The first five blocks contained

S.J. Guastello (✉) • K. Gonring • K. Reiter
Marquette University, Milwaukee, WI, USA
e-mail: Stephen.guastello@marquette.edu

A. Shircel
Kohler Corporation, Sheboygan, WI, USA

M. Malon
Mount Mary University, Milwaukee, WI, USA

P. Timm
Mayo Clinic, Rochester, MN, USA

S.J. Guastello (ed.), *Cognitive Workload and Fatigue in Financial Decision Making*, Evolutionary Economics and Social Complexity Science 13,
DOI 10.1007/978-4-431-55312-0_3

progressively greater complexity which induced greater cognitive load, and the last block was added to induce further fatigue. Separate experimental groups worked at three different speeds. The hypotheses were organized into four groups. The first group was tested by analysis of variance (ANOVA). The latter three were the cusp models for cognitive workload and fatigue. Optimization and risk taking were both analyzed as dependent measures in the ANOVA and cusp models.

1. Optimization would decrease as workload increases. Risk taking would increase as workload increases. Similarly, optimization would decrease and risk taking would increase under more speeded conditions. Based on Conrad (1951), an interaction between speed and load would be expected on both dependent measures.

   Although there was no prior reason to suspect that males and females differ in the susceptibility to cognitive workload and fatigue, gender was also tested as an independent variable because there is a known tendency for males to be more likely to take risks than females (Bem 1974; Zuckerman et al. 1978). Also there was a possibility that the mental calculation task could be more compatible with the interests or comfort zones of males rather than females (Halpern et al. 2007).
2. The cusp models for workload would be better predictors of change in optimization and risk tasking than linear models containing the same variables. The bifurcation variables would be anxiety, PWE, conscientiousness (two separate variables), EI, frustration, anagrams, and GEFT. The asymmetry variables would be speed condition and shifts to a higher level of workload.
3. The cusp models for fatigue would also be better predictors of change in optimization and risk taking than linear models containing the same variables. The bifurcation variables would capture the amount of work accomplished, which was operationalized as the amount of optimization between the starting block of trials and the ending block. The primary group of asymmetry variables would be compensatory abilities: arithmetic, spelling, anagrams, and GEFT. The secondary group of asymmetry variables would be anxiety, PWE, conscientiousness.
4. The cusp analyses just described used comparisons of performance that were taken across blocks of trials from the full range of six blocks; details of this procedure are given in the method section below. Another set of cusp analyses was conducted that compared sequential blocks of trials for workload and fatigue dynamics. This strategy would elaborate the extent to which the different variables for elasticity, load, and compensatory ability would be active throughout the time series. It also provided an opportunity to investigate closer comparisons between workload and fatigue effects over shorter, and gradually longer periods of time. This experimental design technique was used effectively by Stamovlasis (2006, 2011) in some investigations of workload dynamics in chemistry problem solving.

   Another difference in the analyses of sequential blocks was that all six TLX measures were included to determine if subjective ratings would have any explicative value in the workload models beyond the psychosocial variables and speed manipulation already mentioned. For these hypotheses, mental demand, physical demand, and temporal demand were tested as load variables (asymmetry); performance, effort, and frustration were tested as elasticity-rigidity variables (bifurcation).

3.1.1 Method

3.1.1.1 Participants

Participants were 299 undergraduates (mean age = 19.22 years), who were enrolled in psychology courses, of whom 35 % were male. The participants completed a series of tests and a survey before proceeding to the main task, and completed the NASA Task Load Index (TLX) after the main task. The experimental sessions lasted 2.5 h and accommodated small groups of up to 10 participants each.

3.1.1.2 Tests and Measurements

Participants started with 5-min timed tests of arithmetic and spelling abilities, and an untimed survey measuring anxiety, conscientiousness, work ethic, and emotional intelligence. The arithmetic and spelling tests were used in prior studies on cognitive workload and fatigue (Guastello et al. 2012, 2013). Their α reliabilities were .72 and .88 respectively.

The experimental task required mental arithmetic, so the hypothesis that arithmetic test scores would correlate in some way with performance was relatively obvious. The task did not involve spelling words, however. The reason for including the spelling test harkens back to some well-known effects in personnel selection research and education wherein the better performers on computational or spatial tasks scored better on mathematical or spatial skills *and* lower on verbal abilities (Guastello 2002; Guion 1998; Halpern et al. 2007). Good results on a task involving numerical or spatial skills can be attained by people who are high in general intelligence, but not necessarily in math or spatial skills. The winning combination for best results, however, comes from people who have a distinctive abilities in math or spatial visualization. The combination of high-math and low-verbal results is an example of a *suppressor* effect.

The survey measured anxiety, conscientiousness, work ethic, and EI. The anxiety test was a variation of Taylor Manifest Anxiety symptoms (Taylor 1953) that was used in earlier research on cognitive workload and fatigue that was cited in Chap. 2. It consisted of 19 statements such as, "I have nightmares about my job or classes." The participant responded by checking "Agree" (2 points), "?" (1 point), or "Disagree" (0 points). Some items were reverse scored. Alpha reliability was .75.

The EI scale was the 33-item scale developed by Schutte et al. (1998). The participants responded using a 5-point Likert scale; some items were reverse scored here as well (α = .87). An example item was: "When I am faced with obstacles, I remember times when I faced similar obstacles and overcame them."

Conscientiousness was composed of 20 items drawn from the International Personality Item Pool (Goldberg 2011). The items represented the narrower (surface or primary trait) concept of conscientiousness, such as, "I push myself very hard to succeed," and the impulsivity component that is part of the broader definition of the construct, such as, "I do things without thinking of the consequences." The participants responded using a 5-point Likert scale; some items were reverse scored. The impulsivity variable was keyed so that high scores indicated self-control, and low scores indicated impulsivity. The α reliabilities for the broad Conscientiousness construct (20 items), narrow construct (14) items, and impulsivity (6 items) were .88, .83, and .74 respectively. Conscientiousness was used in its narrow form throughout the cusp and linear regression analyses.

The PWE scale consisted of nine items from Buchholz (1977) to which the participant responded by checking "Strongly disagree" = 1, "Disagree" = 2, "?" = 3, "Agree" = 4, or "Strongly Agree" = 5. An example item was: "A person must depend on himself to get ahead." Some items were reverse scored (α = .57).

The GEFT (Witkin et al. 2002) and the mixed anagram test followed the survey. The GEFT items present a simple geometric form and a complex geometric form. The participants were required to locate and trace the simple form that was embedded in the complex form. The GEFT consists of a 2-min timed section of practice items that are not scored, and two 5-min timed groups of 12 items each. The split-half reliability values of the GEFT are .82 based on 177 adults, and .85 based on 150 college students (Witkin et al. 2002).

The mixed anagram test was developed in the lab for this experiment. There were 15 items, each of which consisted of a five-letter word that was scrambled with 5 random digits mixed in. The participant needed to isolate the letters and rearrange them into a word. The vocabulary words for the anagrams were picked from words appearing on the spelling test. The anagram text was delivered in Powerpoint, and participants wrote their responses on an answer sheet. After giving the instructions, the items were presented for 20 s followed by a blank screen for 20 s. The random digits and blank screens were introduced to put some additional demand on memory functions. The alpha reliability for this test was .79.

The TLX scales (Hart and Staveland 1988) were given after the main financial decision task. The participants were simply asked to rate the task on 1–21 scales for mental demand, physical demand, temporal demand, performance level required, effort required, and frustration. The scales do not have verbal anchors associated with the numbers. The frustration scale was the item of interest for the cusp analysis of workload.

3.1.1.3 Financial Decision Task

Participants were given the following instructions: "This experiment is designed to measure your skill at financial investing. For each of the situations that you will be shown, imagine that you have $10,000 to invest in only one of the available options. Imagine further that you have narrowed your investment options to two serious possibilities, which are specified as problem options A and B. You also have a third option C, which is to keep your money in the bank. For all options in all situations, assume that the time for the investment to pay off is 1 year.

"All the information you need to make your decision is given in the statement of options. For each of the situations, mark the letter of your option choice in the space on the answer sheet. You will only have a limited amount of time to make each choice, and it will not be possible to go back to earlier items. Let's try an example: [*An example of a 3-option problem was presented for 30 s, then instructions resumed.*]

"You will probably find that some of the choices are easy to make while others are not so obvious. Do not spend too much time on any one item. Please work without using a calculator. Some scratch paper has been provided, but only the answers on the answer sheet will be counted.

"For items 1–30, assume that these are "no load" investment options, meaning that there is no commission or other similar cost to you for taking part in the investment. Furthermore, there is no risk of losing your investment principal (any part of the original $10,000) from any of the options. For option C in each of the situations, assume that the bank is paying interest at the rate of 4 % per year."

Participants were randomly assigned to one of three speed conditions: 30 s exposure per item, 15 s per item, and 7.5 s per item. The 30 s benchmark was determined from a pilot test in which the participants completed 30 items in paper-and-pencil format without a stated time limit, and most finished within 15 min.

The items were organized into six blocks of items, the first five of which increased in complexity. Examples are shown in Table 3.1. There were 30 items each in blocks 1, 2, and 3, 40 items in block 4, and 45 items in block 5. Only the last 30 items from blocks 4 and 5 were used in the ANOVA and cusp analyses (except the Work Done variable in the fatigue analysis, see below). Participants were shown a brief instruction slide prior to block 2 stating that the hypothetical investments had costs to participate associated with them. Participants were shown a brief instruction slide prior to block 3 stating that the hypothetical investments have both costs to participate and possible losses. No further instruction slides were presented prior to blocks 4, 5, or 6.

The sixth block consisted of 175 items that were the same as the first 175 items but in random order; thus a 5-option item could be followed by a 3-option item, etc. Also the options were randomized relative to their first appearance in the experiment, although the bank option was always the last option. Only the last 30 items from block 6 were used in the ANOVA and cusp analyses (except the Work Done variable).

The goal of the sixth block was to extend the time on task for those who participated in the faster conditions in order to induce enough of a fatigue effect. Thus the participants in the 30 s condition ($n = 54$) only did the first five blocks. For the 15 s condition 62 participants did the first five blocks, and 102 did all six blocks. All participants in the 7.5 s condition ($n = 69$) were presented with all 350 items.

Table 3.1 Sample items

Block 1: 3 options, no load, no stated losses
(a) The potential profit from this investment is $3,000, and the odds are 80 % that the investment will pay off as planned
(b) The potential profit from this investment is $5,000, and the odds are 50 % that the investment will pay off as planned
(c) I would not select either option above, and would keep my money in the bank
Block 2: 3 options, front-end load, no stated losses
(a) The potential profit is $1,000, and the odds of a successful payoff are 90 %, and the load is $200
(b) The potential profit is $8,000, and the odds of a successful payoff are 20 %, and the load is $100
(c) Keep the money in the bank
Block 3: 3 options, front-end load, possible losses stated
(a) The potential profit is $9,000, and the odds of a successful payoff are 40 %, the load is $200, and the chance of losing $500 are 60 %
(b) The potential profit is $1,000, and the odds of a successful payoff are 90 %, the load is $100, and the chance of losing $1,000 are 10 %
(c) Keep the money in the bank which is paying 4 %
Block 4: 4 options
(a) The potential profit from this investment is $2500, and the odds are 40 % that the investment will pay off as planned
(b) The potential profit is $10,000, the odds of a successful payoff are 40 %, the load is $200 and the chances of losing $400 are 50 %
(c) The potential profit is $1,000, the odds of a successful payoff are 90 %, and the cost to participate in the investment is $100
(d) Keep the money in the bank which is paying 3 %
Block 5: 5 options
(a) The potential profit is $2,500, and the odds of a successful payoff are 40 %
(b) The potential profit is $13,000, and the odds of a successful payoff are 40 %, the load is $100 and the chance of losing $5,000 is 50 %
(c) The potential profit is $11,000, and the odds of a successful payoff are 20 %, and the load is $100
(d) The potential profit is $18,000 and the odds of a successful pay off are 30 %
(e) Keep the money in the bank which is paying 3 %

The procedure did not give participants any feedback or paid incentives for several reasons: First many investment evaluations like these are made in a short amount of time without feedback during the process. Second, feedback would interrupt the cognitive processes that were underway. The laboratory tasks for prior studies in cognitive workload and fatigue varied to the extent that feedback was built into the task itself. Third, feedback conditions would require a lot of delay time to compute the optimizing levels to produce a financial reward, which would also artificially disrupt the fatigue effect.

3.1.1.4 Analyses

Each item on the financial task produced a correct answer for the optimizing scale and an answer toward the risk taking scale. The raw scores were corrected for guessing given that the blocks contained different numbers of options. The two dependent measures were analyzed separately.

There were four ANOVA analyses, all of which were split-plot designs. In the first two analyses for optimizing and risk taking, the repeated factor was the scores on the first five blocks, which represented the complexity of the decision. Gender (two levels) and speed condition (three levels) were between-subjects effects. In the second two analyses, the repeated factor was the scores on all six blocks, and the fixed factors were gender (two levels) and speed condition (two levels).

The cusp analyses were polynomial regression analogues of Eq. 2.2:

$$\Delta z = \beta_0 + \beta_1 z_1^3 + \beta_2 z_1^2 + \beta_3 b z_1 + \beta_4 a \tag{3.1}$$

where z was the dependent measure observed at two points in time, b was the bifurcation variable, a was the asymmetry variable, and all variables were transformed by location and scale before entering into the regression model (Guastello 1995, 2011, 2013), and are thus designated as z instead of y. Location was the lowest observed value of y, and scale was its standard deviation. Multiple variables could be entered as b or a, and they would have separate regression weights associated with them. The quadratic element is actually optional; its significance indicates that catastrophic shifts in one direction outnumber shifts in the opposite direction. If statistical significance was not obtained for the cubic or bifurcation terms in the model, which are more important for characterizing the unique dynamics of the cusp, the quadratic term would be dropped.

R^2 for the cusp model was compared with R^2 for two linear comparison models:

$$\Delta y = \beta_0 + \beta_1 b + \beta_2 a, \tag{3.2}$$

$$y_2 = \beta_0 + \beta_1 y_1 + \beta_2 b + \beta_3 a. \tag{3.3}$$

The linear models involve the same variables that are used as cusp control variables but without the nonlinear structures. Equation 3.2 describes a prediction of change in the dependent measure. Equation 3.3 describes the subsequent performance as a function of prior performance and the research variables. The R^2 for the cusp models should exceed the R^2 for their linear counterparts, although if the two are equal it is sufficient to conclude that the cusp was a better explanation because of the qualitative dynamical features that it offers compared to linear models.

If R^2 for the cusp exceeded R^2 for Eq. 3.2, then the cusp would explain changes in performance better than the linear model. If R^2 for the cusp exceeded R^2 for the pre-post linear model (Eq. 3.3), then it is possible to conclude that the cusp was the dominant explanation for performance variance. If on the other hand, R^2 for the pre-post model exceeded R^2 for the cusp, then one concludes that the linear function for non-change was a better description of the events in the data set than the cusp.

Workload There were four cusp analyses, two for workload and two for fatigue. The optimizing score for workload at time 1 was the optimizing score on block 1. For time 2, the participants were randomly assigned to one of four conditions, in which the time 2 score would be either the score on block 2, 3, 4, or 5. The condition produced a new variable, *workload*, which was also corrected for location and scale, and tested as an asymmetry variable. The experimental condition for speed produced another new variable with three levels that was also tested as an asymmetry variable. The bifurcation variables tested were frustration, PWE, EI, conscientiousness, impulsivity, anagrams, and anxiety. The backward elimination procedure for multiple regression was used for all cusp and linear comparison analyses. The process was repeated for risk taking.

Fatigue The optimizing score for workload at time 1 was also the optimizing score on block 1. For time 2, however, the score was either the score on block 5 or 6, depending on whether the participant was in the 175-item or a 350-item condition. The bifurcation variables were speed condition, and work done. *Work done* was the number of correct optimizing responses given on blocks 2–4 or 2–5. This measure included the 25 items that were not used in the scores for the blocks 4 or 5, and the 145 items that were not used to make the optimizing score for block 6 (if the participant was in an experimental condition that required the use of block 6). The asymmetry variables were scores on arithmetic, spelling, GEFT, anagrams, conscientiousness, impulsivity, anxiety, and EI. For fatigue and risk taking, work done was the same measurement used in the analysis for optimizing. The same rule was used to define risk taking at time 1 and time 2. The other bifurcation and asymmetry variables were the same.

Sequential Blocks Cusp models were reconstructed to compare blocks 1 with 2, 1 with 3, 1 with 4, and 1 with 5. For blocks that contained more than 30 trials, only the last 30 were used. TLX rating were included as control variables in the workload model as described above: mental, physical, and temporal demands as asymmetry variables; and performance effort, and frustration as bifurcation variables.

The asymmetry variable for the workload models was speed condition; which will be a measure of workload. It was not possible to use the "workload" (complexity of the optimization problem) variable from the previous analyses because there was only one workload condition that affected all participants in each blockwise comparison.

Speed condition was a bifurcation variable in the fatigue models comparing blocks 1 and 2, as there was no intervening block of trials between the time 1 and time 2 measurements. It was possible to include performance on intervening trials for the comparisons between blocks 1 and 3–6, however.

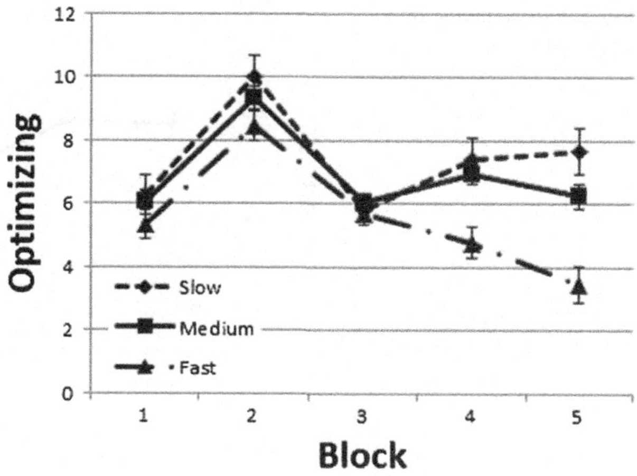

Fig 3.1 Optimizing results by workload block and speed condition

3.1.2 Results

3.1.2.1 ANOVA

The results for optimizing in the five-block design revealed significant main effects for speed ($F(2, 281) = 5.757$, $p < .01$, $\eta_p^2 = .039$), load ($F(4, 1124) = 39.520$, $p < .001$, $\eta_p^2 = .123$), and the speed-by-load interaction ($F(8, 1124) = 2.929$, $p < .01$, $\eta_p^2 = .020$). The polynomial trend analyses showed significant effects for the linear ($F = 15.511$, $p < .001$), quadratic ($F = 16.042$, $p < .001$), cubic ($F = 98.582$, $p < .001$), and fourth-order ($F = 56.172$, $p < .001$) effects, which meant that all sequential differences in means were significant; see Fig. 3.1. The other interactions were not statistically significant.

The shift from block 1 to 2 showed an improvement in optimizing when load increased by introducing a varying cost to participate in the investment. This is a counterintuitive effect that is probably explained as a practice or automaticity effect. The shift from block 2 to 3 showed a decline in optimizing when load increased by introducing varying possible losses. This sub-optimization is an expected result from increased load. The shift from block 3 to 4 showed some improvement in optimizing for the slow and medium speed conditions, which was probably a practice effect again. Performance in the fast condition dropped sharply, however. Optimizing declined from block 4 to 5 where load increased again.

The results for risky choices in the five-block design revealed a significant main effect for load only ($F(4, 1124) = 24.177$, $p < .001$, $\eta_p^2 = .079$). The polynomial trend analyses showed significant effects for the linear ($F = 15.511$, $p < .001$), quadratic ($F = 23.183$, $p < .001$), cubic ($F = 9.887$, $p < .01$), and fourth-order ($F = 51.291$, $p < .001$) effects, which meant that all sequential differences in means were significant (Fig. 3.2). The other interactions were not significant. There was an increase in risk taking from block 1 to 2, which is consistent with

Fig. 3.2 Risk taking by workload block

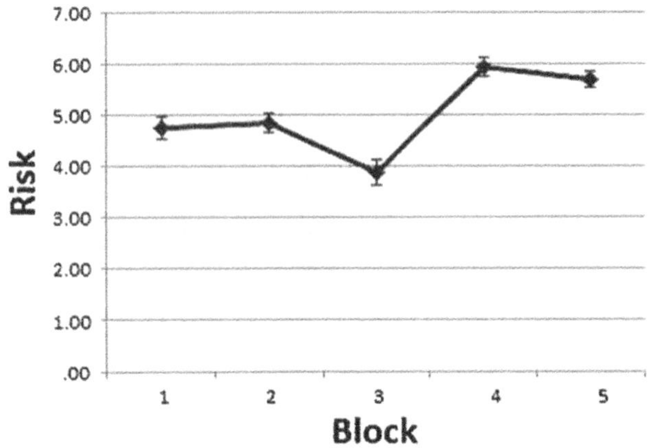

stress-risk principle. Risky choices dropped from block 2 to 3, however, indicating an increase in sub-optimality or loss-averse responses. Risky choices increased again from blocks 3 to 4, then dropped again at block 5.

The results for optimizing in the six-block design with only two levels of speed revealed a significant main effect for load only ($F(5, 835) = 23.185$, $p < .001$, $\eta_p^2 = .122$). The polynomial trend analyses showed significant effects for the linear ($F = 17.879$, $p < .001$), cubic ($F = 85.973$, $p < .01$), fourth-order ($F = 9.361$, $p < .01$) and fifth-order ($F = 17.408$, $p < .001$) effects, which meant that all sequential differences in means were significant (Fig. 3.3). Although the gender-by-load interaction was not significant overall, there was a difference in the cubic-level trends between genders ($F(1, 835) = 7.028$, $p < .01$). It appeared that the females experienced more of a load effect than the males at blocks 4 and 5. The other interactions were not statistically significant.

The results for risky choices in the six-block design revealed a significant main effect for load only ($F(5, 835) = 13.105$, $p < .001$, $\eta_p^2 = .073$). The polynomial trend analyses showed significant effects for the linear ($F = 3.808$, $p < .10$), quadratic ($F = 9.639$, $p < .001$), cubic ($F = 34.944$, $p < .001$), fourth-order ($F = 3.801$, $p < .10$) and fifth-order ($F = 15.586$, $p < .001$) effects, which meant that all sequential differences in means were significant (Fig. 3.4). There was a tiny three-way interaction between speed, load, and gender ($F = 1.888$ $p < .10$, $\eta_p^2 = .010$). The other interactions were not significant. Because of the small size and intermittent and obscure nature of the gender effects, gender effects were not pursued further.

3.1.2.2 Cusp Models for Workload

The workload cusp for optimizing contained all the necessary components to support a cusp: the cubic structure, bifurcation variables, and asymmetry variables ($R^2 = .389$, $F(6, 269) = 17.221$, $p < .001$; Table 3.2). The bifurcation variables that corresponded to greater rigidity were low conscientiousness and high self-control.

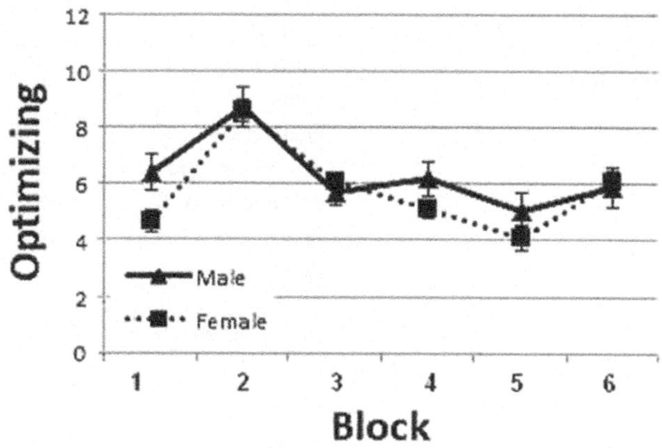

Fig. 3.3 Optimizing by workload block and gender

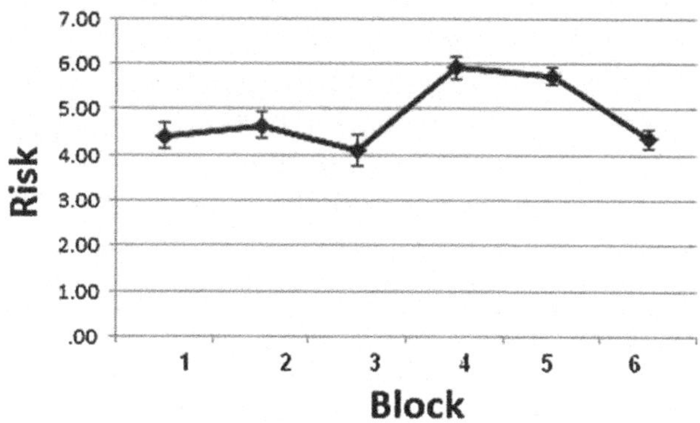

Fig. 3.4 Risk taking by workload block with fatigue condition

Speed and load were the two asymmetry variables corresponding to vertical load. Relative improvements in performance resulted from smaller increases in load and working in the slower conditions.

The cusp model for workload was also more accurate than the two alternative linear models. The linear difference model difference model contained only one significant variable, which was load ($R^2 = .090$, $F(3, 272) = 9.480$, $p < .001$). The parameters for the backward elimination regression were set to remove a variable if its $p > .15$. The criterion for statistical significance was $p < .10$, so non-significant variables were occasionally left in the models as in this case. According to the pre-post linear model ($R^2 = .358$, $F(5, 270) = 15.090$, $p < .001$), optimizing performance was better at time 2 if it was also better at time 1, conscientiousness was lower, self-control high, speed slower, and load increases smaller.

The workload cusp for risky choices also contained all the necessary components to support a cusp ($R^2 = .251$, $F(6, 270) = 15.110$, $p < .001$; Table 3.3). The bifurcation variables corresponding to greater rigidity were higher work ethic, and the field dependence cognitive style as indicated by lower scores on the GEFT. Load was the only asymmetry variable; increases in risky choices occurred if the change in load was less, and risk-averse choices resulted from increased load.

Table 3.2 Cusp and linear models for workload, optimizing

Variable	β	*t*
Cusp, $R^2 = .389$		
Cubic	.89	2.985***
Quadratic	−1.401	−4.378****
z_1*conscientiousness	−.229	−2.190**
z_1*impulsivity	.244	2.470**
Speed	−.083	−1.693*
Load	−.322	−6.651****
Linear difference, $R^2 = .090$		
EI	−.093	−1.528
Impulsivity	.094	1.532
Load	−.286	−4.889****
Linear pre-post, $R^2 = .358$		
Optimizing block 1	.462	9.442****
Conscientiousness	−.137	−1.834*
Impulsivity	.152	2.061**
Speed	−.079	−1.562
Load	−.322	−6.529****

*$p < .10$, **$p < .05$, ***$p < .01$, ****$p < .001$

Table 3.3 Cusp and linear models for workload, risk taking

Variable	β	*t*
Cusp, $R^2 = .251$		
Cubic	.996	3.461***
Quadratic	−1.129	−3.799***
z_1*frustration	−.098	−1.576
z_1*work ethic	.147	2.250**
z_1*GEFT	−.138	−2.147*
Load	−.375	−7.049***
Linear difference, $R^2 = .179$		
GEFT	−.128	−2.300**
Conscientiousness	.174	2.128**
Impulsivity	−.122	−1.473
Work ethic	.093	1.641
Load	−.376	−6.703****
Linear pre-post, $R^2 = .250$		
Risk taking block 1	.375	7.044****
Arithmetic	−.084	−1.588
Conscientiousness	.143	1.809*
Impulsivity	−.154	−1.957*
Load	−.314	−5.896****

*$p < .10$, **$p < .05$, ***$p < .01$, ****$p < .001$

The workload cusp for risk predicted change in risky choices better than the linear difference model ($R^2 = .179, F(5, 271) = 11.792, p < .001$). Increases in risky choices were greater if conscientiousness and PWE were higher, and self-control and change in load were lower (greater impulsivity). The accuracy of the pre-post model for risky choices was equivalent to that of the cusp model ($R^2 = .250$, $F(5, 270) = 10.709, p < .001$). Risk taking was greater at time 2 if it was also greater at time 1, conscientiousness was higher, self-control lower, and change in load was less.

3.1.2.3 Cusp Models for Fatigue

The fatigue cusp for optimizing contained all the necessary components to support a cusp ($R^2 = .557$, $F(5, 277) = 6.737, p < .001$; Table 3.4). The bifurcation variables promoting greater changes in performance in both directions were greater speed and greater amounts of work done in between the time 1 and time 2 measuring points. The compensatory ability was GEFT; performance improved over time for individuals with field independent cognitive styles.

The cusp model for fatigue and optimizing was more accurate than either of the linear alternatives. The linear difference model contained only the speed variable ($R^2 = .038$, $F(1, 275) = 10.954$, $p < .001$). The pre-post model contained three variables ($R^2 = .236$, $F(3, 273) = 28.076$, $p < .001$). Risk taking at time 2 was greater to the extent that it was greater at time 1, GEFT scores were higher, and the work pace was faster.

The fatigue cusp for risky choices also contained all the necessary components to support a cusp ($R^2 = .439$, $F(6, 276) = 36.029$), $p < .001$; Table 3.5). The bifurcation variables promoting greater changes in risk taking in both directions were greater speed and getting *less* work done in between the time 1 and time 2 measuring points. The compensatory abilities were GEFT and anagram scores, both of which were negatively weighted. Increases in risk taking were more likely for people who were field dependent and performed poorly on the anagrams test.

The cusp model for fatigue and risk taking was more accurate than either of the linear alternatives. The linear difference model contained six variables ($R^2 = .205$, $F(6, 270) = 11.582, p < .001$). Risk taking increased under conditions of fatigue for those who scored lower on GEFT (field dependent), anagrams, and EI. Risk taking also increased for those who scored higher on conscientiousness, lower on self-control (impulsive), and worked under faster conditions. The pre-post linear model contained a similar result ($R^2 = .266$, $F(6, 269) = 9.880$, $p < .001$).

3.1.2.4 Graphic Illustration

As a further illustration of the dynamical character of the performance trends, Fig. 3.5 shows a time series of optimizing and risk taking behavior, for one participant each. The charts were produced by taking the time series of

Table 3.4 Cusp and linear models for fatigue, optimizing

Variable	β	t
Cusp, $R^2 = .557$		
Cubic	1.076	4.583****
Quadratic	−2.709	−10.361****
z_1*speed	.17	3.881****
z_1*work done	1.192	12.945****
GEFT	.073	1.793*
Linear difference, $R^2 = .038$		
Speed	.196	3.310****
Linear pre-post, $R^2 = .236$		
Optimizing block 1	.448	8.382****
GEFT	.088	1.649*
Speed	.167	3.156**

*$p < .10$, **$p < .05$, ***$p < .01$, ****$p < .001$

Table 3.5 Cusp and linear models for fatigue, risk taking

Variable	β	t
Cusp, $R^2 = .439$		
Cubic	1.414	5.318****
Quadratic	−1.638	−5.633****
z_1*speed	.325	5.392****
z_1*work done	−.421	−7.279****
GEFT	−.078	−1.689*
Anagrams	−.126	−2.763**
Linear difference, $R^2 = .205$		
GEFT	−.145	−2.629***
Anagrams	−.127	−2.294**
EI	−.107	−1.789*
Conscientiousness	.222	2.551**
Impulsivity	−.139	−1.696*
Speed	.323	5.646****
Linear pre-post, $R^2 = .266$		
Risk taking block 1	.104	1.973**
GEFT	−.105	−1.976**
Anagrams	−.094	−1.755*
Conscientiousness	2.359	−.019**
Impulsivity	−.176	−2.225**
Speed	.429	7.826****

*$p < .10$, **$p < .05$, ***$p < .01$, ****$p < .001$

350 observations, dividing them into aggregates of five stimulus items, plotting a score on a 1–5 scale, and detrending the resulting series of 70 observations. Further information about nonlinear analyses that can be afforded by this detrending strategy is presented in Chap. 5. Fluctuations to the left of the central axis were

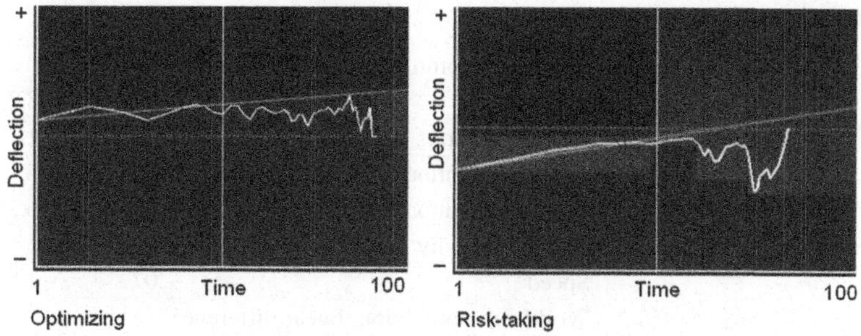

Fig. 3.5 Detrended time series for optimizing and risk taking, one participant each

instigated by experimental blocks 1–5 in which workload was increased. Fluctuations to the right of the central axis came from block 6 where the workload per item was randomized. All participants (in the 350 item condition) showed a similar pattern with a clump of variability toward the end of the time series, which is expected from a fatigue process. The most common variation in the charts were overall upward or downward trends and whether the final burst of variability ended on an uptick or a downtick.

3.1.2.5 Cusp Models by Block

Block 2 The results for the cusp and linear models for block 1 versus block 2 appear in Table 3.6. The cusp model for workload and optimizing was more accurate ($R^2 = .633$, adj $R^2 = .624$ $F(6, 262) = 75.164$, $p < .001$) than the two linear alternatives, and contained all the essential components. Frustration, both the narrow and broad definitions of conscientiousness, and impulsivity were significant bifurcation variables. People who were more conscientious in the narrow definition and more self-controlled showed smaller changes in performance as the workload increased. There appeared to be a suppressor effect relationship between conscientiousness in the broad sense and the two components. Alternatively, two subgroups of participants may have been represented by that combination of variables. Participants who worked in the faster speed conditions showed smaller changes in optimizing as workload increased. The linear difference model contained only one variable, which was emotional intelligence ($r^2 = .015$, $F(1, 267) = 3.939$, $p < .05$); participants higher in EI showed less change as workload increased. The linear pre-post model contained two variables, which were optimizing on block 1 and anagrams ($R^2 = .504$, adj. $R^2 = .500$, $F(2, 273) = 138.701$, $p < .001$); both variables were positively correlated with optimizing on block 2. Apparently people who scored better on the anagrams test experienced less impact on the change in workload.

The cusp model for workload and risk taking was more accurate ($R^2 = .593$, adj $R^2 = .585$, $F(5, 263) = 76.501$, $p < .001$) than the two linear alternatives, and

Table 3.6 Cusp and linear models for blocks 1 vs 2

Variable	β	t
Workload, optimizing, cusp		
$z_1{}^3$	.704	18.233****
z_1 × frustration	.083	1.752*
z_1 × conscientiousness (broad)	2.932	6.144****
z_1 × conscientiousness (narrow)	−2.082	−6.259****
z_1 × impulsivity	−1.099	−5.702****
Speed	−.07	−1.830*
Workload, optimizing, linear difference		
Emotional intelligence	−.121	−1.985**
Workload, optimizing, pre-post linear		
Optimizing block 1	.696	16.428****
Anagrams	.08	1.867*
Workload, risk taking cusp		
$z_1{}^3$	.739	18.656****
z_1 × work ethic	−.124	−2.169**
z_1 × conscientiousness (broad)	.998	1.996**
z_1 × conscientiousness (narrow)	−.686	−1.931*
z_1 × impulsivity	−.422	−2.091**
Workload, risk taking, pre-post linear		
Risk block 1	.601	12.360****
Fatigue optimizing, cusp, $z_1{}^3$	.759	18.693****
Frustration	.085	2.103**
Conscientiousness (narrow)	.076	1.884*
Fatigue, optimizing, linear difference		
Emotional intelligence	−.117	−1.915*
Fatigue optimizing, pre-post linear		
Optimizing block 1	−.399	−7.041****
Anagrams	.107	1.887*
Fatigue, risk taking, cusp		
$z_1{}^3$	.734	17.627****
Fatigue risk taking linear difference		
Arithmetic	−.115	−1.839*
Fatigue risk taking, linear pre-post		
Risk taking block 1	.619	12.839****
Arithmetic	−.085	−1.759*

*$p < .10$, **$p < .05$, ***$p < .01$, ****$p < .001$

contained the most essential components. Significant effects were obtained for the cubic term and bifurcation variables, which defined the shape of the surface. The bifurcation variables were work ethic and the same configuration of conscientiousness and impulsivity. People scoring higher on work ethic showed smaller changes in performance in response to workload, which is consistent with the rigidity hypothesis. The speed effect was not significant as a bifurcation variable in this model. The linear difference for workload and risk taking was null ($R^2 = .000$). The pre-post linear model for workload and risk taking contained only one variable, which was risk taking in block 1 ($r^2 = .361$, $p < .001$).

The cusp model for fatigue and optimizing was more accurate than the two linear alternatives ($R^2 = .573$, adj $R^2 = .568$, $F(3, 264) = 117.961$, $p < .001$). It contained the cubic term, and two asymmetry variables, which were frustration and the narrow version of conscientiousness. A bifurcation effect was not found; speed condition apparently did not contribute to fatigue between the first two blocks of trials. Only one variable contributed to the linear difference model, which was emotional intelligence ($r^2 = .014$, $F(1, 266) = 3.669$, $p < .10$). Two variables contributed to the linear pre-post model, which were optimizing at time 1 and scores on the anagram test ($R^2 = .161$, adj. $R^2 = 1.55$ $F(2, 265) = 133.796$, $p < .001$).

The cusp model for fatigue and risk taking was more accurate than the two linear alternatives ($r^2 = .539$, $F(1, 266) = 310.712$, $p < .001$). It only contained the cubic model and was not a sufficiently complete model. The linear difference model contained only one variable, which was arithmetic test scores ($r^2 = .013$, $F(1, 266) = 3.578$, $p < .10$). The linear pre-post model contained two variables, which were optimizing at time 1 and arithmetic ($R^2 = .385$, adj $R^2 = .381$, $F(2, 265) = 83.100$, $p < .001$).

Block 3 The results for the cusp and linear models for block 1 versus 3 appear in Table 3.7. The cusp model for workload and optimizing was more accurate ($R^2 = .528$, adj. $R^2 = .523$ $F(3, 465) = 98.961$, $p < .001$) than the two linear alternatives. The bifurcation variables were the same configuration of the two conscientiousness measures and impulsivity as reported for block 2. The cubic and asymmetry terms were missing, however, so what was actually obtained was a moderating effect of conscientiousness and impulsivity (self-control) with the time 1 performance measure. The linear difference model for workload and optimizing contained one variable, which was the scores on the anagram test ($r^2 = .020$, $F(1,267) = 5.416$, $p < .05$). The pre-post linear model also contained only one variable, which was mental demand ($r^2 = .014$, $F(1, 275) = 3.875$, $p < .10$).

The cusp model for workload and risk taking was also missing the cubic term ($R^2 = .168$, adj. $R^2 = .156$ $F(4, 264) = 13.374$, $p < .001$). The bifurcation variables were the same configuration of the two conscientiousness measures and impulsivity measures as reported for optimizing between blocks 1 and 3. The asymmetry variable was scores on the GEFT; field independent people tended to reduce risk taking. The linear difference model contained two variables, which were the GEFT (negative weight again) and conscientiousness-narrow ($R^2 = .036$, adj. $R^2 = .029$ $F(2, 266) = 4.934$, $p < .01$); the latter weight was positive indicating that conscientious participants were actually taking greater risks. The pre-post linear model contained only one variable which was risk taking on block 1 ($r^2 = .116$ $F(1, 275) = 36.239$, $p < .001$).

The cusp model for fatigue and optimizing also did not contain a cubic term ($R^2 = .035$, adj. $R^2 = .027$ $F(2, 265) = 4.762$, $p < .05$). There was an interaction effect, however between work done during the intervening interval and optimizing

Table 3.7 Cusp and linear models for blocks 1 vs 3

Variable	β	*t*
Workload, optimizing, cusp		
$z_1 \times$ conscientiousness (broad)	5.088	10.843****
$z_1 \times$ conscientiousness (narrow)	−3.757	−11.583****
$z_1 \times$ impulsivity	−2.052	−10.842****
Cubic and asymmetry missing		
Workload, optimizing, linear difference		
Anagrams	−.141	−2.327
Workload, optimizing, pre-post linear		
Mental demands	.117	1.958*
Workload, risk taking cusp		
$z_1 \times$ conscientiousness (broad)	2.521	3.132***
$z_1 \times$ conscientiousness (narrow)	−1.569	−2.734***
$z_1 \times$ impulsivity	−1.162	−3.708****
Embedded figures test	−.174	−2.128**
Workload, risk taking, linear difference		
Embedded figures test	−.149	−2.465**
Conscientiousness (narrow)	.104	1.719*
Workload, risk taking, pre-post linear		
Risk taking block 1	.341	−6.020****
Fatigue optimizing, cusp		
$z_1 \times$ work done	−.136	−2.256**
Anagrams	−.121	−2.006**
Fatigue, optimizing, linear difference		
Anagrams	−.127	−2.090**
Fatigue, risk taking, cusp		
$z_1{}^3$	−.145	−2.939***
$z_1 \times$ work done	−.633	−12.823****
Fatigue risk taking linear difference		
Embedded figures test	−.15	−2.474**
Conscientiousness (narrow)	.102	1.686*
Fatigue risk taking, linear pre-post		
Work done	.193	3.209****
Embedded figures test	−.17	−2.816***

*$p < .10$, **$p < .05$, ***$p < .01$, ****$p < .001$

at time 1. The asymmetry variable was the anagram test; people scoring higher on the test improved less than others, or declined more, as workload increased. The linear difference model contained one variable, which was anagrams ($r^2 = .016$, $F(1, 266) = 4.367$, $p < .05$). The pre-post model, however, was null ($r^2 = .000$).

The cusp model for fatigue and risk taking contained the cubic term and work done as the bifurcation term ($R^2 = .383$, adj. $R^2 = .378$, $F(2, 265) = 82.247$, $p < .001$); the asymmetry variable was missing. The linear difference model contained two variables, GEFT and conscientiousness narrowly defined

($R^2 = .036$, adj $R^2 = .028$, $F(2, 265) = 4.906$, $p < .01$). The linear pre-post model also contained two variables, GEFT and work done ($R^2 = .057$, adj $R^2 = .050$, $F(2,265) = 8.019$, $p < .001$).

Block 4 The results for the cusp and linear models for block 1 versus 4 appear in Table 3.8. The cusp model for workload and optimizing was more accurate ($R^2 = .374$, adj. $R^2 = .359$, $F(6, 262)$, $p < .001$) than the two linear alternatives, and all parts were present. There were four bifurcation variables: conscientiousness broad and narrow, impulsivity, and GEFT; field independent people were more rigid as workload increased. Speed was the asymmetry variable, performance decreased when work pace was faster. There were four significant effects in the linear difference model ($R^2 = .043$, adj $R^2 = .029$, $F(4, 264)$ 2.976, $p < .01$): GEFT (positive, field independence improved performance), conscientiousness narrowly defined (negative), impulsivity (positive, denoting self-control), and work speed (negative). There were six significant effects in the linear pre-post model ($R^2 = .341$, adj. $R^2 = .326$, $F(6,270) = 23.262$, $p < .001$); people who performed better in block 4 also performed better at block 1, worked in the slower condition (s), rated the performance demand lower than others, rated the physical demand higher, were less conscientious (rigid) in the narrow definition, and were less impulsive.

The cusp model for workload and risk taking was relatively weak and not as accurate as the linear pre-post model ($R^2 = .111$, adj. $R^2 = .098$, $F(4, 264) = 13.374$, $p < .001$). The cubic term was present along with three bifurcation variables. Conscientiousness broad and narrow and impulsivity were configured the same way here as they were in cusp models reported to this point. The asymmetry variable was missing. The linear difference model contained two significant effects: GEFT and work ethic ($R^2 = .026$, adj. $R^2 = .019$, $F(2, 266) = 3.064$, $p < .01$). The pre-post linear model contained three significant effects ($R^2 = .214$ adj. $R^2 = .205$, $F(3, 274) = 24.734$, $p < .001$); people who increased risk taking reported higher physical demands, lower performance demands, and took more risks in block 1. The conclusion for this set of analyses is that changes in performance were more gradual and proportionate to the independent variables than they were catastrophic and sudden.

The cusp model for fatigue and optimizing was well formed ($R^2 = .182$, adj $R^2 = .167$, $F(5, 262) = 11.691$, $p < .01$), containing the cubic term, work done as the bifurcation term, and three compensatory abilities: GEFT, conscientiousness narrow, and impulsivity. The cusp was less accurate than the linear pre-post model, however. The linear difference model contained three variables: GEFT, conscientiousness narrow, and impulsivity ($R^2 = .031$, adj. $R^2 = .020$, $F(3, 264) = 2.859$, $p < .05$). The linear pre-post model contained four variables: optimizing in block 1 and GEFT, conscientiousness narrow, and impulsivity again ($R^2 = .310$, adj $R^2 = .299$ $F(4, 263) = 29.493$, $p < .001$). The conclusion for this set of analyses is again that changes in performance were gradual and proportionate to the independent variables than they were catastrophic and sudden.

The cusp model for fatigue and risk taking only contained the bifurcation variable, work done ($r^2 = .157$ $F(1, 266) = 49.401$, $p < .001$). Even so, it was still

Table 3.8 Cusp and linear models for blocks 1 vs 4

Variable	β	*t*
Workload, optimizing, cusp,		
z_1^3	.243	4.821****
z_1 × conscientiousness (broad)	4.541	6.443****
z_1 × conscientiousness (narrow)	−3.621	−.259****
z_1 × impulsivity	−1.497	−5.404****
z_1 × embedded figures	.214	3.013***
Speed	−.114	−2.278**
Workload, optimizing, linear difference		
Embedded figures	.105	1.736*
Conscientiousness (narrow)	−.182	−1.970**
Impulsivity	.174	1.909*
Speed	−.109	−1.760*
Workload, optimizing, pre-post linear		
Optimizing block 1	.451	−9.039****
Speed	−.138	−2.656***
TLX performance demands	−.153	−3.007***
TLX physical demands	.185	3.667****
Conscientiousness (narrow)	−.227	−2.764***
Impulsivity	.215	2.444**
Workload, risk taking cusp		
z_1^3	−.116	−1.944*
z_1 × conscientiousness (broad)	3.078	4.763****
z_1 × conscientiousness (narrow)	−2.075	−4.637****
z_1 × impulsivity	−1.271	−4.876****
Workload, risk taking, linear difference		
Embedded figures	−.115	−1.898*
Work ethic	.119	1.967**
Workload, risk taking, pre-post linear		
TLX physical demand	.098	1.814*
TLX performance demand	−.132	−2.442**
Risk taking block 1	.428	7.965****
Fatigue optimizing, cusp		
z_1^3	.34	6.026****
z_1 × work done	−.184	−3.198***
Embedded figures	.14	2.441**
Conscientiousness (narrow)	−.217	−2.556**
Impulsivity	.231	2.737***
Fatigue, optimizing, linear difference		
Embedded figures	.102	1.676*
Conscientiousness (narrow)	−.216	−2.384**
Consc. impulsivity	.198	2.176**

(continued)

Table 3.8 (continued)

Variable	β	*t*
Fatigue optimizing, pre-post linear		
Optimization block 1	.468	9.026****
Embedded figures	.176	3.371****
Conscientiousness (narrow)	−.261	−3.397****
Consc. impulsivity	.222	2.884***
Fatigue, risk taking, cusp		
z_1 × work done	−.396	−7.029****
Fatigue, risk taking linear difference		
Anagrams	−.109	−1.794*
Conscientiousness (narrow)	.126	2.076**
Fatigue, risk taking, pre-post linear		
Optimization block 1	.305	5.196****
Frustration	.103	1.770*
Embedded figures	−.126	−2.137**

*$p < .10$, **$p < .05$, ***$p < .01$, ****$p < .001$

more accurate than the alternative models. The linear difference model contained two significant effects: anagrams and conscientiousness narrowly defined ($R^2 = .028$, adj .021 $F(2, 265) = 3.802$, $p < .05$). The linear pre-post model contained three significant effects: risk taking at block 1, frustration, and GEFT scores ($R^2 = .109$, adj $R^2 = .099$, $F(3, 264) = 10.770$, $p < .001$). By the time the participants reached block 4, those who rated greater levels of frustration began to take more risks.

Block 5 The results for the cusp and linear models for block 1 versus 5 appear in Table 3.9. The cusp model for workload and optimizing was well formed ($R^2 = .322$, adj $R^2 = .309$, $F(5, 263) = 24.976$, $p < .001$), although it was not as accurate as the linear pre-post model. The cusp contained significant effects for the cubic term, three bifurcation variables, and speed as the asymmetry variable. The three bifurcation variables were once again conscientiousness broad and narrow and impulsivity. The linear difference model contained three significant effects: conscientiousness broad and narrow and impulsivity ($R^2 = .062$, adj $R^2 = .052$, $F(3,265) = 5.878$, $p < .001$). The linear pre-post model contained five significant effects: optimizing at block 1, speed, TLX performance demands, conscientiousness narrowly defined, and impulsivity ($R^2 = .402$, adj. $R^2 = .391$, $F(5, 271) = 36.429$, $p < .001$). Once again the conclusion for this set of analyses is again that changes in performance were more gradual and proportionate to the independent variables than they were catastrophic and sudden.

The cusp model for workload and risk taking was also well-formed ($R^2 = .233$, adj. $R^2 = .219$, $F(5, 263) = 16.010$, $p < .001$), and this time it was more accurate than the two linear alternatives. Significant effects in the cusp model were the cubic

Table 3.9 Cusp and linear models for blocks 1 vs 5

Variable	β	t
Workload, optimizing, cusp		
z_1^3	.136	2.604*
$z_1 \times$ conscientiousness (broad)	3.46	6.054****
$z_1 \times$ conscientiousness (narrow)	−2.842	−7.219****
$z_1 \times$ impulsivity	−1.047	−4.515****
Speed	−.192	−3.689****
Workload, optimizing, linear difference		
Conscientiousness (broad)	−.196	−2.154**
Conscientiousness (narrow)	.222	2.479**
Speed	−.175	−2.872***
Workload, optimizing, pre-post linear		
Optimizing block 1	.52	10.978****
Speed	−.167	−3.449****
TLX performance demands	.185	3.874****
Conscientiousness (narrow)	−.186	−2.563**
Impulsivity	.197	2.768**
Workload, risk taking cusp		
z_1^3	−.095	−1.707*
$z_1 \times$ conscientiousness (broad)	4.062	6.683****
$z_1 \times$ conscientiousness (narrow)	−2.705	−6.462****
$z_1 \times$ consc. impulsivity	−1.793	−7.270****
Speed	−.103	−1.871*
Workload, risk taking, linear difference		
Embedded figures test	−.128	−2.113*
Conscientiousness (narrow)	.219	2.385**
Impulsivity	−.162	−1.784*
Anagrams	−.132	−2.138**
Speed	−.106	−1.713*
Workload, risk taking, pre-post linear		
TLX performance demands	.187	3.283***
Risk taking block 1	.428	7.965****
Fatigue optimizing, cusp		
z_1^3	−.18	3.085****
$z_1 \times$ work done	−.285	−4.916***
Conscientiousness (narrow)	−.257	−3.029***
Impulsivity	.255	3.029***
Fatigue, optimizing, linear difference		
Conscientiousness (narrow)	−.251	−2.774***
Impulsivity	.252	2.782***

(continued)

Table 3.9 (continued)

Variable	β	*t*
Fatigue optimizing, pre-post linear		
Optimization block 1	.535	10.719****
Embedded figures test	.086	1.708*
Anagrams	.082	1.659*
Conscientiousness (narrow)	−.274	−3.723****
Impulsivity	.26	3.521****
Fatigue, risk taking, cusp		
$z_1 \times$ work done	−.578	11.558****
Fatigue risk taking linear difference		
Embedded figures test	−.135	−2.212**
Anagrams	−.144	−1.896*
Conscientiousness (narrow)	.197	2.184**
Impulsivity	−.159	−1.760*
Fatigue, risk taking, pre-post linear		
Speed	−.107	−2.008**
Risk taking block 1	.428	7.545****
Work done	−.421	−7.323****

*$p < .10$, **$p < .05$, ***$p < .01$, ****$p < .001$

term and the same bifurcation and asymmetry variables that were part of the workload and optimization cusp. The linear difference model contained five significant effects: GEFT, conscientiousness narrow, impulsivity, anagrams and speed ($R^2 = .058$, adj. $R^2 = .040$ $F(5, 263) = 3.252$, $p < .05$); participants who increased their risk taking tended to be field dependent, more conscientious, more impulsive, worked at the slower speeds, and did not score as highly on the anagrams test. The linear pre-post model contained only two significant effects: risk taking on block 1 and performance demands ($R^2 = .112$, adj. $R^2 = .106$ $F(2, 274) = 17.356$, $p < .001$); participants who rated the performance demands of the task higher took more risks from blocks 1 to 5.

The cusp model for fatigue and optimizing contained all the necessary parts ($R^2 = .167$, adj. $R^2 = .155$, $F(3, 263) = 13.211$, $p < .001$), but it not as accurate as the linear pre-post model. Significant effects were obtained for the cubic term, work done, conscientiousness narrowly defined and impulsivity. The linear difference model contained two effects, conscientiousness narrow and impulsivity ($R^2 = .032$, adj $R^2 = .025$ $F(2, 265)$ 4.423, $p < .05$). The linear pre-post model ($R^2 = .368$, adj. $R^2 = .356$ $F(5, 262) = 30.500$, $p < .001$) contained the latter two variables plus optimizing at block 1, GEFT, and anagrams. Once again the conclusion for this set of analyses is that changes in performance were more gradual and proportionate to the independent variables than they were catastrophic and sudden.

The cusp model for fatigue and risk taking contained only one variable, which was the bifurcation effect for work done ($r^2 = .334$ $F(1, 266) = 133.587$, $p < .001$).

Table 3.10 Summary of block-wise comparisons, R^2 for cusp, linear difference, and pre-post linear models

Comparison	Cusp	Linear difference	Linear pre-post
Workload, optimizing			
Blocks 1 vs 2	.633	.015	.504
Blocks 1 vs 3	.528	.02	.014
Blocks 1 vs 4	.374	.043	.341
Blocks 1 vs 5	.322	.062	.402
Average	*.464*	*.035*	*.315*
Workload risk taking			
Blocks 1 vs 2	.593	0	.361
Blocks 1 vs 3	.168	.036	.214
Blocks 1 vs 4	.111	.026	.112
Blocks 1 vs 5	.233	.058	.215
Average	*.276*	*.04*	*.226*
Fatigue, optimizing			
Blocks 1 vs 2	.573	.014	.161
Blocks 1 vs 3	.035	.016	0
Blocks 1 vs 4	.182	.031	.31
Blocks 1 vs 5	.167	.032	.368
Average	*.239*	*.023*	*.21*
Fatigue risk taking			
Blocks 1 vs 2	.539	.013	.385
Blocks 1 vs 3	.383	.036	.057
Blocks 1 vs 4	.153	.028	.109
Blocks 1 vs 5	.334	.051	.223
Average	*.352*	*.032*	*.194*

Ironically it was more accurate than the two alternatives models. The linear difference model contained four effects: GEFT, anagrams, conscientiousness narrow, and impulsivity ($R^2 = .051$, adj $R^2 = .036$ $F(4, 263) = 3.498$, $p < .001$). The linear pre-post model contained three effects: speed, risk taking at block 1 and work done ($R^2 = .223$, adj $R^2 = .215$, $F(3, 282) = 27.040$, $p < .001$). The effect size for the interactive relationship between earlier performance and work done (bifurcation variable) was greater than the two additive effects observed in the pre-post model.

Table 3.10 summarizes the R^2 coefficients for the cusp and linear alternative models for the four different block comparisons. The largest advantage for the cusp was obtained for fatigue and risk taking (16 % of the variance accounted for), followed by workload and optimizing (14 %). Thus roughly one third of the variance accounted for by the cusp models is attributable to the nonlinear process itself.

Table 3.11 Final cusp model, workload, optimizing with subjective ratings

Variable	β	t
z_1^3	.824	2.934***
z_1^2	−1.488	−5.224****
$z_1 \times$ TLX performance	.206	2.862***
Speed	−.092	1.900*
Load	−.298	−6.080****

*$p < .10$, **$p < .05$, ***$p < .01$, ****$p < .001$

3.1.2.6 Final Workload Model

The analyses for the workload cusps that were presented earlier based on blocks 1–5 were repeated, but this time the TLX ratings of subjective workload were included as potential bifurcation and asymmetry variables. This analysis would provide a competitive test of the psychosocial variables versus subjective ratings. Once again the regression method of backward elimination was used. The results for optimizing appear in Table 3.11. The nuance was that the TLX Performance scale substituted for conscientiousness and impulsivity; the accuracy of the model was about the same, however ($R^2 = .386$, adj $R^2 = .374$, $F(5, 263) = 33.053$, $p < .001$). There were no substitutions or additional variables found for workload and risk taking, however. Analogous models for fatigue were not conducted because subjective ratings of workload were not part of the fatigue theory.

3.1.3 Discussion

The results of the study should be interpreted from four different focal points: cognitive biases, the dynamics of workload and fatigue, the contributing cognitive abilities or psychosocial variables, and the sequential analysis of blocks.

3.1.3.1 Stress, Risk and Reflection Effects

Optimizing performance was affected by work speed, load, and their interaction, which is consistent with the traditional findings (Conrad 1951). The speed effect was only apparent when the slowest experimental condition was present in the ANOVA analyses, however. The slowest condition (30 sec/frame) produced the best performance results. Some of the experimental participants did complain about the slowness. The amount of time per frame was apparently necessary for the participants to do a good job, although the machine-driven timing could have produced a source of stress by itself (Hancock 2007; Guastello et al. 2013).

Risk taking was affected by load stress but not speed stress. Load stress sometimes produced reflection effects, however. These findings contrast with those summarized in Slovic and Peters (2006) concerning time pressure, possibly because the time pressure experiments that they examined were more pressurized than ours, or because the task was framed differently. Rather than asking participants to evaluate whether they would support an innovation in isolation from other innovations, our participants were asked to make comparative evaluations of their options.

The results of the present study were consistent with those of Porcelli and Delgado (2009) concerning stress, risk taking, and the reflection effect. Blocks 1 and 2 of the present experiment, which produced an increase in risk taking, that was comparable to their gain domain construct which produced comparably more risk taking. Blocks 3, 4, and 5 of the present experiment contained possible losses of different severities combined with the possible gains. The gains and losses were not homogenously large or small across items or options within stimuli in the present study, which seems realistic for many real-world decision environments. Risk taking dropped at first then increased, whereas optimization improved or reduced depending on the level of speed stress. The reflection effect occurred in the cases where both optimization and risk taking took downturns.

3.1.3.2 Workload Effects

The cusp models for workload that were based on blocks 1–5 together were not *much* more accurate than the next best linear comparison models, but they were strong enough and complete enough to support the cusp interpretation for workload phenomena. It is only necessary for the nonlinear model to be as good as the linear alternative; the qualitative explanation afforded by the dynamics adds value to the understanding of the phenomenon.

Importantly, some of variables that were supposed to function as vertical load or rigidity-flexibility did so. Both speed and decision complexity corresponded to vertical load (asymmetry) in the optimization model, and decision complexity (only) worked for risk taking.

The bifurcation variables representing rigidity versus elasticity were different results for optimization and risk taking. For optimization, low conscientiousness and high self-control (low scores on the impulsivity scale) produced larger changes upward and downward as load increased. Frustration, PWE, and GEFT produced the bifurcation effect for risk taking.

3.1.3.3 Fatigue Effects

The fatigue effect that was built on the full spectrum of data was greater than the workload effect, evidenced by the difference in R^2 coefficients between cusp and linear alternative models. Fatigue models accommodate both the drop in performance associated with being tired and the increase in performance associated with the warm-up effect. The speed stress variable, which represented the number of stimuli processed in a given amount of time, and the amount of work done, which was the actual number of correct optimizations between the start and end points, acted as the bifurcation variables that separated those who lost work capacity and those who experienced the exercise effect. The bifurcations variables were the same for both optimization and risk taking.

The asymmetry parameter in fatigue models consists of compensatory abilities. Arithmetic, which should be directly related to optimizing performance, was not part of the fatigue model. GEFT, however, was part of both the cusp and linear models; people who scored higher on GEFT (field independent), demonstrated greater optimization and less risk taking. Anagrams were negatively weighted in the risk taking model, indicating that people who took more risks under fatiguing conditions were less creative, or not as proficient in fluid intelligence as those who controlled the risk-taking tendency.

The foregoing pattern of results indicates that the abilities that are more likely to be helpful in a fatigue process are compensatory rather than direct. Abilities drawn from the fluid domain also appear to be more viable than those from the crystallized domain as initially suspected. It is possible that the fluid abilities afford more mental degrees of freedom to compensate fatigue, but this speculation requires much further research.

The psychosocial variables did not contribute to the asymmetry parameter in either fatigue model. EI, conscientiousness, and impulsivity did contribute to the linear models for fatigue and risk taking, however. Conscientiousness and impulsivity were prominent bifurcation variables in the early stages of the experiment, but gave way to other effects later on. The impact of the psychosocial variables are discussed further below.

3.1.3.4 Constructs

The abilities that are compensatory in the fatigue model and the variables that reflect rigidity versus elasticity vary across situations in which the workload and fatigue models have been assessed to date. In the present context, arithmetic was not a significant contributor to the workload or fatigue models, even though it had good face value for performance on the task itself. Spelling, which is a verbal ability, did not have any relevance to fatigue in financial decision making. The suppressor effect that we were anticipating in the present study did not occur. The spelling test has now been tested in a few different contexts, and only once did it show up as a compensatory variable in one of the seven perceptual-motor tasks (Guastello et al. 2013). Verbal abilities from the fluid intelligence domain might have more impact in future studies, particularly if the experimental tasks were more verbally demanding than the ones that have been studies thus far. A verbally demanding task in the financial arena might involve trolling through news reports to find pertinent information that could affect the future value of investments.

Field independence is a new addition to the battery of constructs being tested as elasticity-rigidity or compensatory ability variables. It is the ability to separate figure from ground in the sense of Gestalt psychology of perception, or disentangle perceptual elements, but it also represents a cognitive style or strategy for separating critical elements from noncritical ones in more abstract contexts (Stamovlasis and Tsaparlis 2012; Witkin et al. 2002). This ability probably explains how field independent people make greater use of their available channel capacity – they do not expend mental resources on extraneous data. In the present study, field independence acted as a compensatory ability for fatigue: Field independent people showed improvement in optimization performance over time and a decrease in risk taking. This point by itself warrants further exploration as a simple predictor of performance in financial professions. Witkin et al. (2002) noted, however, that the GEFT only correlates with performance in a perceptual task if the task involves isolating a target from irrelevant material.

GEFT scores also acted as a bifurcation variable in the workload model for risk taking. People who were field *de*pendent would increase or decrease risk taking under increasing load conditions. The field independent people would be more likely to target critical information and mentally discard the additional chatter.

Anagrams were introduced as a measure of fluid intelligence that was not directly related to working memory capacity. People who scored higher on anagrams took smaller increases in risks under conditions of fatigue (but not for workload). The reason for this selective effect requires further exploration. Once can speculate, however, that anagram test scores, which are usually associated with creativity, are detecting people who have a higher tolerance for ambiguity, which is another common characteristic of creative people. As such they would be less reactive to the odds of success that were stated in each option. This explanation needs to be studied directly in future research.

The nexus of EI, anxiety, and frustration played only a small role in this study. Anxiety now seems to become more relevant in a challenging social context (Guastello et al. 2012; Ladouceur et al. 2009; Naber et al. 2015) than in the condition operating here. Anxiety was not a significant contributor to either the workload or fatigue models. The same was true for EI, except that EI showed a small effect in the linear difference model for risk taking and fatigue. Frustration found a home as a bifurcation variable in the workload model for risk taking; this finding was consistent with an effect reported earlier in the workload model for the vigilance task (Guastello et al. 2014).

The nexus of conscientiousness, impulsivity versus self-control, and PWE produced some interesting results. Perhaps the most interesting finding was that when conscientiousness was separated from the broad definition that is usually invoked in the FFM into two constructs, the narrow version of conscientiousness and self-control versus impulsivity, both variables were relevant to optimization and risk taking, but in opposite directions. High conscientiousness, which denotes attentiveness to details, precision, and following rules, was paired with impulsivity in the case of risk taking under increasing workload and fatigue, and low conscientiousness was paired with self-control in the case of optimization under increasing workload.

PWE appeared as a bifurcation variable in the cusp model for risk taking under workload. Those higher in workload were likely to increase *or* decrease risk as workload increased, compared to people who scored lower on that variable. This finding is consistent with the theoretical premise that PWE represents a form of adaptive rigidity similar to conscientiousness.

3.1.3.5 Block by Block Analyses

One of the premises of the two-cusp model of workload and fatigue is that the effects of each can be separated by a sufficiently complex experimental design that permits the testing of the two models simultaneously. This premise played out differently in the previous applications and the full-data models just discussed. Specifically, the workload model assigned participants to different blocks for the time 2 measurements up to block 5, and the fatigue model assessed the trend that spanned blocks 1–6. The analyses of sequential blocks assessed both the workload and fatigue models as time unfolded from bock to block.

Another idea that was introduced in the analysis of sequential blocks was the inclusion of TLX ratings as asymmetry and bifurcation variables in the workload model. The premise behind the use of subjective ratings in the human factors literature is that the effects of workload would register cognitively before an adaptive action was taken that would have the effect of keeping performance consistently up the criterion.

The analyses provided some new and interesting results that supplemented the full-spectrum models. First the R^2 coefficients for the cusp models were strongest for comparisons between blocks 1 and 2, possibly because there was more room for learning effects. Some participants caught on to the task faster than other did, but once they did, they were less influenced by increases in workload during the middle periods. They reacted more strongly again as workload reached the last stage.

Second, the results showed a gradual introduction of some of the constructs such as PWE and TLX ratings as more time on task elapsed. Arithmetic ability appeared early on then phased out. TLX ratings, particularly frustration, phased in on block 4. TLX ratings were made only once at the end of the experimental session, and ratings are known to be sensitive to recency effects; events that occur closest to the time of the ratings have more influence on the ratings than earlier events. Ratings were not introduced earlier in the session after separate blocks of trials because the task switching could have undermined the fatigue effect that was expected to be building up.

The third interesting finding occurred when the workload model was re-analyzed to include the TLX ratings. Here we saw that the ratings of performance levels required to do the job substituted for the conscientiousness and impulsivity (self-control) constructs. The substitution provides a good connection between the personality characteristics of the people who see greater performance demands with a work situation. It also conveys which aspect of workload ratings corresponds to the trait combination that is thought to explain higher levels of work performance across many types of jobs: Conscientious employees see a greater demand in the situation and work accordingly. Those who cannot see the demand cannot work towards it so well. Further connections between the ability variables and TLX ratings are studied in the next chapter.

3.1.3.6 Limitations and Future Research

The present study had some limitations that offer new opportunities for future research, some of which have been mentioned already. Inasmuch as most real-world financial transactions are electronically mediated in some form, the problem of stress and cognitive bias are human factors problems as well. Now that the complex relationships among stress, risk taking and the reflection effect have become apparent, a new group of questions arises concerning the design of software and information displays that financial analysts use and how different design features impact on cognitive biases. Ideally the equipment should minimize the opportunity for stress from workload and the role individual differences (e.g. in personality or cognitive style) in the operation of such systems. It is an open question, however, whether program trading offloads the stress from the human operator to the machine, or just transforms the stress into different concerns about the reliability of the internal algorithms.

The options were presented to the participants in this study on one slide, so there was no ambiguity as to which option should be compared against which other option. In real-world situations, the time-phasing of the options that a decision maker might want to consider is irregular over time, such that relevant comparisons could be separated by minutes, days, or even weeks; the presence of absence of an option during a given time frame could change the perceived utilities of the options that are available. This is an important facet of satisficing in the face of bounded rationality: There is only so much information that can be processed during a time interval, and a decision needs to be made within a time constraint. External memory aids might help the real-world decision maker, but at present the efficacy of the existing support software has not been ascertained.

Regarding time-phased information, a possible new direction for continued research on workload and fatigue would be to consider *N*-back tasks. In an N-back task, the participant is shown a series of stimuli and make a response if a stimulus is the same as the one appearing one stimulus earlier (1-back), two stimuli earlier (2-back) and so on. N-back tasks are particularly demanding on working memory (Kane and Engle 2002), and are thus interesting for their fatigue potential. Workload and fatigue in *N*-back tasks have been studied recently through the cusp catastrophe paradigm using generic stimuli such as letters of the alphabet, geometric shapes, and cartoon faces (Guastello et al. 2015); a similar study with financial data has not been tackled yet. As one might anticipate, asking a participant to hold more stimuli in working memory (e.g. 3-back versus 2-back) adds a considerable amount of cognitive workload and quickens fatigue.

Another gap between the experiment and the real world is the manner in which the expected payoff and odds of payoff were established for each option. In the experiment, they were stated clearly in the problem stimuli. In the real world, the investors must ascertain those pieces of information for themselves, and it would not be surprising if the determination of expected payoff or odds of payoff were distorted by some of the known forms of bias.

Investors' strategies, which were not addressed here, could play a role in the perception of risk and payoff as well. Fundamentalists, speculators, beauty contest judges, and noise traders (Rosser 1997) would probably evaluate things differently, and would probably place different emphases on the time between the purchase and the payoff. Variables related to these trading strategies were not included in this experiment. Issues related to portfolio management and leveraging risks are another class of variables that could affect the interpretation of risks and rewards. We do make some progress in attacking the issue of profiling in Chap. 7.

In some of the previous experiments with the cusp paradigm, the workload effect was stronger than the fatigue effect, and the recommendation was to extend the work time to produce the fatigue effect. In the present study the opposite occurred, and the evidence thus suggested that the range of workload demands could have been greater, especially in the slow speed condition. Future research designs should place greater demands on the working memory capacity.

The present study made some progress finding rigidity-elasticity variables associated with optimization and risk taking. The search continues, however, for others that reflect the participants' flexibility for making changes in their cognitive strategies.

References

Bem, S. L. (1974). The measurement of psychological androgyny. *Journal of Consulting and Clinical Psychology, 42*, 155–162.

Buchholz, R. A. (1977). The belief structure of managers relative to work concepts measured by a factor analytic model. *Personnel Psychology, 30*, 567–587.

Conrad, R. (1951). Speed and load stress in a sensorimotor skill. *British Journal of Industrial Medicine, 8*, 1–7.

Goldberg, L. (2011). *International personality item pool*. Retrieved September 30, 2011, from http://ipip.ori.org

Guastello, S. J. (1995). *Chaos, catastrophe, and human affairs: Applications of nonlinear dynamics to work, organizations, and social evolution*. Hillsdale: Lawrence Erlbaum Associates.

Guastello, S. J. (2002). *Managing emergent phenomena: Nonlinear dynamics in work organizations*. Hillsdale: Lawrence Erlbaum Associates.

Guastello, S. J. (2011). Discontinuities: SETAR and catastrophe models with polynomial regression. In S. J. Guastello & R. A. M. Gregson (Eds.), *Nonlinear dynamical systems analysis for the behavioral sciences using real data* (pp. 251–280). Boca Raton: CRC Press.

Guastello, S. J. (2013). Catastrophe theory and its applications to I/O psychology. In J. M. Cortina & R. Landis (Eds.), *Frontiers of methodology in organizational research* (pp. 29–62). New York: Routledge.

Guastello, S. J., Boeh, H., Schimmels, M., Gorin, H., Huschen, S., Davis, E., Peters, N. E., Fabisch, M., & Poston, K. (2012). Cusp catastrophe models for cognitive workload and fatigue in a verbally-cued pictorial memory task. *Human Factors, 54*, 811–825.

Guastello, S. J., Boeh, H., Gorin, H., Huschen, S., Peters, N. E., Fabisch, M., & Poston, K. (2013). Cusp catastrophe models for cognitive workload and fatigue: A comparison of seven task types. *Nonlinear Dynamics, Psychology, and Life Sciences, 17*, 23–47.

Guastello, S. J., Malon, M., Timm, P., Weinberger, K., Gorin, H., Fabisch, M., & Poston, K. (2014). Catastrophe models for cognitive workload and fatigue in a vigilance dual-task. *Human Factors, 56*, 737–751.

Guastello, S. J., Reiter, K., Malon, M., Timm, P., Shircel, A., & Shaline, J. (2015). Catastrophe models for cognitive workload and fatigue in N-back tasks. *Nonlinear Dynamics, Psychology, and Life Sciences, 19*, 173–200.

Guion, R. M. (1998). *Assessment, measurement, and prediction for personnel decisions*. Hillsdale: Lawrence Erlbaum Associates.

Halpern, D. F., Benbow, C. P., Geary, D. C., Gur, R. C., Hyde, J. S., & Gernsbacher, M. A. (2007). The science of sex differences in science and mathematics. *Psychological Science in the Public Interest, 8*(1), 1–51.

Hancock, P. A. (2007). On the process of automation transition in multitask human-machine systems. *IEEE Transactions on Systems, Man, and Cybernetics – Part A: Systems and Humans, 37*, 586–598.

Hart, S. G., & Staveland, L. E. (1988). Development of the NASA task load index (TLX): Results of experimental and theoretical research. In P. A. Hancock & N. Meshkati (Eds.), *Human workload* (pp. 138–183). Amsterdam: North-Holland.

Kane, M. J., & Engle, R. W. (2002). The role of prefrontal cortex in working-memory capacity, executive attention, and general fluid intelligence: An individual-differences perspective. *Psychonomic Bulletin & Review, 9*, 617–671.

Ladouceur, C. D., Silk, J. S., Dahl, R. E., Ostapenko, L., Kronhaus, D. M., & Phillips, M. L. (2009). Fearful faces influence attentional control processes in anxious youth and adults. *Emotion, 9*, 855–864.

Naber, A. M., McDonald, J. N., Asenuga, O. A., & Arthur, W., Jr. (2015). Team members' interaction anxiety and team training effectiveness: A catastrophic relationship? *Human Factors, 57*, 163–176.

Porcelli, A. J., & Delgado, M. R. (2009). Acute stress modulates risk taking in financial decisions. *Psychological Science, 20*, 278–283.

Rosser, J. B., Jr. (1997). Speculations on nonlinear speculative bubbles. *Nonlinear Dynamics, Psychology, and Life Sciences, 1*, 275–300.

Schutte, N. S., Malouf, J. M., Hall, L. E., Haggerty, D. J., Cooper, J. T., Golden, C. J., & Dornheim, L. (1998). Development and validation of a measure of emotional intelligence. *Personality and Individual Differences, 25*, 167–177.

Slovic, P., & Peters, E. (2006). Risk perception and affect. *Current Directions in Psychological Science, 15*, 322–325.

Stamovlasis, D. (2006). The nonlinear dynamical hypothesis in science education problem solving: A catastrophe theory approach. *Nonlinear Dynamics, Psychology and Life Science, 10*, 37–70.

Stamovlasis, D. (2011). Nonlinear dynamics and neo-Piagetian theories in problem solving: Perspectives on a new epistemology and theory development. *Nonlinear Dynamics, Psychology and Life Science, 15*, 145–173.

Stamovlasis, D., & Tsaparlis, G. (2012). Applying catastrophe theory to an information-processing model of problem solving in science education. *Science Education, 96*, 392–410.

Taylor, J. A. (1953). A personality scale of manifest anxiety. *Journal of Abnormal and Social Psychology, 48*, 285–290.

Witkin, H. A., Oltman, P. K., Raskin, E., & Karp, S. A. (2002). *A manual for the embedded figures test* (2nd ed.). Palo Alto: Consulting Psychologists Press.

Zuckerman, M., Buchsbaum, M. S., & Murphy, D. L. (1978). Sensation seeking and its biological correlates. *Psychological Bulletin, 88*, 187–214.

Chapter 4
Individual Differences in the Assessment of Cognitive Workload

Stephen J. Guastello

Abstract This chapter addresses a problem that is salient in the human factors and ergonomics communities regarding the inconsistent connections between subjective ratings of workload and actual performance. Previous work with vigilance tasks showed that a substantial part of subjective workload, and further connections to actual performance, were associated with psychosocial variables related to elasticity as defined in the cusp catastrophe models for cognitive workload and fatigue. The empirical study presented in this chapter was conducted with the data set described in earlier chapters. The influence of cognitive variables, compared to psychosocial variables, is much stronger in financial decision making contexts. It now appears that context is highly relevant for determining which psychosocial or ability variables best explain individual differences in subjective ratings of workload, all situational variables considered equal. Context, furthermore, affects the combination of psychosocial variables, abilities, and subjective ratings that result in performance dynamics.

4.1 Introduction

Psychology made the transition from a branch of philosophy to an experimental science in 1879 when Wilhelm Wundt established the first experimental psychology laboratory in Leipsig. The earliest era of experimental psychology was dominated by questions concerning what topics should be studied and how. One of the first counterpoints developed between Wundt and his first U.S. student, James McKeen Cattell (unrelated to R. B. Cattell of personality theory fame mentioned earlier). Wundt wanted to identify and clarify the cognitive phenomena that characterized the whole human race. J. M. Cattell wanted to focus on individual differences in cognition or most anything else (Boring 1950).

S.J. Guastello (✉)
Marquette University, Milwaukee, WI, USA
e-mail: Stephen.guastello@marquette.edu

S.J. Guastello (ed.), *Cognitive Workload and Fatigue in Financial Decision Making*, Evolutionary Economics and Social Complexity Science 13,
DOI 10.1007/978-4-431-55312-0_4

Although both perspectives generated uncountable contributions to their credit, a distinct separation in perspective still remains in the study of cognitive processes. For instance one can troll through stacks of articles on working memory and find only occasional mention of personality and other individual differences being examined; individual differences that have been studied most often involve age differences and impact of different types of pathologies. Theoreticians have called attention to this deficit (Corr 2010), and numerous researchers have started to do something about it (Gruszka et al. 2010). Some focus on individual differences in decision strategies (Wilhelms and Reyna 2015; De Neys and Osman 2014), and others on the role of emotion, which can either enhance or impair rational decision making (Blanchette 2014). Stress can be a source of disruptive emotion, as mentioned already. The implications for the further understanding of cognitive biases and bounded rationality should be obvious, although there is still much to be learned. The EI construct of from previous chapters was specifically intended to bridge the cognitive and emotional aspects of mental life. It became very popular among human resource professionals because it addressed a widespread question of what makes some people are better than others at recognizing emotional events within themselves or other people and making helpful responses. It was not a prominent variable in the study reported in Chap. 3, but it has been an effective predictor of performance when interaction with other people was involved (Guastello et al. 2015).

Human factors engineering (ergonomics) remained shy about individual differences until relatively recently (Karwowski 2000). The underlying assumption for many years is that better systems are not susceptible to any influence from individual differences; they should work fine for everyone. Part of the reason for thinking that way is that the system operators were already selected by the employers, which is matter completely out of the hands of people designing software and equipment. This thinking has changed now that many systems are being made for use by wide segments of the population, and contemporary systems are becoming more complex involving many people working together.

4.2 Psychosocial Variables, TLX Ratings, and Performance

One such study of individual differences that is particularly relevant to the present project assessed the connection between psychosocial variables and ratings of cognitive workload on the NASA TLX scales (Guastello et al. 2015). Four psychosocial variables were selected for study because of their theoretical role as elasticity-rigidity constructs: conscientiousness, PWE, anxiety and EI. The 141 participants performed two tasks simultaneously. One task was to watch a security camera (a virtual reality program) and ring a bell when they saw an intruder. The second task was to assemble a jigsaw puzzle. The participants either worked alone or with another participant. Ratings were given as the end of the experiment session for the whole dual-task experience. People scoring higher in anxiety reported more temporal demand (time pressure) and frustration than others. People scoring higher in work ethic also reported more frustration. People scoring higher on emotional intelligence reported higher performance demands and effort required compared to others.

Performance was measured as the miss error rate for the full 90 min video sequence and by the number of puzzle pieces assembled. There was only one measurement for each task; measurements were not segmented into specific time units as they were done in Chap. 3. There were fewer miss errors if the participants worked in pairs, and more errors recorded for those scoring higher in conscientiousness and work ethic. More puzzle pieces were assembled if the participants worked in pairs, and rated the performance demands higher; fewer pieces were assembled by those scoring higher in work ethic and by those rating the physical demands higher. The finding concerning PWE was a bit of a mystery that has not yet been solved.

Interaction effects were tested between EI and working in pairs for each of the dependent measures. The hypothesis was that emotional intelligence would have more impact if the participants were working in pairs where the influence of the other people might require some response. There were two such effects for TLX ratings. The correlation between emotional intelligence and ratings of temporal demand was positive for people working in pairs, but negative for those working alone. Similarly, the correlation between emotional intelligence and ratings of effort required was positive for people working in pairs, but negative for people working alone. No interaction effects were found for the two performance measures. The same hypotheses were tested for anxiety and working in pairs, but no interaction effects were found.

Conscientiousness, when used in the broad definition had little direct correlation between ratings or performance. When the measure was separated into the narrow definition of conscientiousness and impulsivity-control, some new results were obtained. The narrowly defined conscientiousness measure was negatively correlated with miss errors and ratings of temporal demand. People who scored higher toward self-control rated the temporal demands as greater, however.

4.3 Cognitive Abilities, TLX Ratings, and Performance

Having reviewed the previous experience with the psychosocial variables, ratings and performance, the remainder of this chapter reports the findings for cognitive abilities, ratings of workload, and performance on the financial decision task. The cognitive variables were arithmetic, spelling, and GEFT. Two features of the experiment were included: work speed (three levels), and whether the participant received 175 stimuli or 350 stimuli. (Some participants in the medium speed condition received 175 stimuli and some received 350). Gender was also included as an independent variable.

The main data analyses were organized into two sets. One set used cognitive and experiment-specific variables and gender as independent variables predicting TLX ratings. The second set used the same independent variables plus TLX ratings to predict optimizing performance on the first 175 items, optimizing on all 350 items, risk taking on the first 175 items, and risk taking on all 350 items. Stepwise multiple regression was used throughout to produce a competitive test of the variables. The goal of the analyses was to find the smallest set of variables that could explain the most variance in outcomes. They were essentially competitive tests of the variables that were involved.

Descriptive statistics for the research variables appear in Table 4.1 along with t-tests that compared males' and females' scores. Compared to males, the females rated the mental demands of the task greater, physical demand less, performance demands greater, and frustration higher. There were no gender differences on ability or performance measurements.

Correlations among the TLX variables appear in Table 4.2. The three strongest relationships were between mental demands and temporal demands, mental demands and effort, and performance and effort. Also of interest, the correlation between risk taking and optimizing was 0.32 ($p < 0.001$) for the 175-stimulus set, and 0.20 ($p < 0.01$) for the 350 stimulus set.

Stepwise multiple regression analyses for the TLX scales as the dependent variables appear in Table 4.3. Participants who rated the physical demands higher worked in the slower speed condition and scored more field dependence on the GEFT ($R = 0.284$, adj. $R^2 = 0.074$, $F(2, 276) = 12.150$, $p < 0.001$). Participants who rated the temporal demand higher worked in the faster speed conditions, were more often female, scored relatively lower on the arithmetic test and higher on the spelling test. ($R = 0.350$, adj. $R^2 = 0.110$, $F(4, 279) = 9.715$ $p < 0.001$).

Table 4.1 Descriptive statistics by gender

	Full	Sample	Males		Females		
Variable	M	SD	M	SD	M	SD	t
Arithmetic	13.85	5.26	13.50	5.39	14.29	5.12	−1.23
Spelling	25.93	8.99	26.10	8.84	26.07	9.12	0.27
GEFT	10.96	4.97	11.31	5.31	10.84	4.79	0.76
TLX							
Mental	13.73	4.16	12.86	4.27	14.28	4.06	−2.81**
Physical	4.00	4.70	4.60	4.83	3.72	4.65	1.53**
Temporal	11.88	5.77	10.68	5.61	12.75	5.41	1.53
Performance	11.57	4.31	12.92	3.86	10.73	4.43	−3.09***
Effort	12.33	4.63	12.42	4.89	12.32	4.48	0.18
Frustration	13.45	5.62	12.36	4.89	14.32	5.39	−2.92**
Performance							
Risky 175	18.58	13.03	19.13	14.36	18.57	12.40	0.35
Risky 350	21.27	15.65	23.66	12.36	20.11	13.43	1.40
Optimize 175	77.54	15.90	78.86	17.08	76.54	15.57	0.76
Optimize 350	130.41	28.76	134.80	31.92	128.27	26.97	1.40

**$p < 0.01$, ***$p < 0.001$

Table 4.2 Correlations among TLX scales

Variable	2	3	4	5	6
1. Mental	0.12*	0.51***	−0.06	0.46***	0.25***
2. Physical		0.02	−0.09	0.09	0.19***
3. Temporal			−0.02	0.43***	0.24***
4. Performance				0.24***	−0.22***
5. Effort					0.06
6. Frustration					

*$p < 0.05$, **$p < 0.01$, ***$p < 0.001$

Table 4.3 Stepwise multiple regression for TLX scales as dependent measures with abilities and gender

Variable	β	*t*	R^2
Physical demand			
Embedded figures	−0.236	−4.091***	0.056
Speed	−0.157	−2.729**	0.081
Temporal demand			
Speed	0.202	3.566***	0.055
Gender	0.174	3.067**	0.080
Arithmetic	−0.154	−2.728**	0.100
Spelling	0.151	2.682**	0.122
Performance demand			
Gender	−0.238	−4.178***	0.061
Embedded figures	0.196	3.448***	0.099
Frustration			
Gender	0.158	2.715**	0.029
Duration (set length)	0.126	2.157*	0.045

*$p < 0.05$, **$p < 0.01$, ***$p < 0.001$

Participants who rated the performance demand higher tended to be male and more field independent ($R = 0.315$, adj. $R^2 = 0.093$, $F(2, 278) = 15.358$, $p < 0.001$). Participants who reported higher levels of frustration tended to be in the 350-item task condition and female ($R = 0.211$, adj. $R^2 = 0.038$, $F(2, 285) = 6.665$, $p < 0.001$). No significant effects for individual differences were found for mental demand or effort.

Stepwise multiple regression analyses for optimization and risk taking as the dependent variables appear in Table 4.4. There was only one predictor for optimization on the 175-item set, which was that those who performed better scored more field independent on the GEFT ($r = 0.383$, $p < 0.001$). The results changed for the 350-item set, however, for which there were two predictors; performance was better at the middle speed level (15 s/stimulus) and for those who rated the effort demand higher ($R = 0.256$, adj. $R^2 = 0.054$, $F(2, 166) = 5.823$, $p < 0.01$).

There was only one variable correlated with risk taking on the 175-item set. Those who took more risks were those who rated the performance demand for the task higher ($r = 0.139$, $p < 0.05$). There was also only one variable correlated with

Table 4.4 Stepwise multiple regression for optimization and risky choices with TLX scales, abilities, and gender

Variable	β	t	R^2
Optimizing 175			
Embedded figures	0.383	4.424***	0.146
Optimizing 350			
Speed	−0.198	−2.633**	0.036
TLX effort	0.172	2.293*	0.066
Risky choices 175			
TLX performance	0.139	2.260*	0.019
Risky choices 350			
Embedded figures	−0.171	−2.093*	0.029

$^{*}p<0.05$, $^{**}p<0.01$, $^{***}p<0.001$

risk taking on the 350-item set. Those who took more risks were more field dependent ($r=-0.171$, $p<0.05$).

4.4 Discussion

The NASA TLX ratings of subjective workload have been widely used for comparing tasks and equipment designs. It would stand to reason that the ratings would be affected by aspects of the task that should, in principle, affect workload. The presentation speed did affect two of the ratings, and the number of stimuli processed during the work period affected frustration levels.

The 1–21 scoring system that was used here was taken from the downloadable form from the NASA (n.d.) website. Some investigators use a 0–100 scale for comparing tasks; a mental demand score and a total performance score above 50 is considered very difficult (Warm et al. 2008). The six ratings shown in Table 4.1 can be converted to the 0–100 scale by subtracting 1 and multiplying the result by 5. The total score is the unweighted average of the six converted ratings (Nygren 1991). Thus for the full sample, the converted mean for mental demand is 63.65, and the converted total is 50.80. Both values indicate a very high level of cognitive workload. It would be probably be valuable for future research to compare these ratings with those taken from different tasks performed by real-world financial experts and advisors.

Subjective cognitive workloads should be less for people who have stronger task-related abilities. The cognitive ability measures did affect three of the ratings, notably temporal demand or felt time pressure. Abilities, if correctly identified should correlate with performance as well. Here the field independence pole of the GEFT was associated with optimizing on the 175-item set and field dependence was associated with risk taking on the 350-item set.

Although more research is needed to determine if a generalizable pattern actually exists, the present results plus those reported by Mykytyn (1989) strongly suggest that field independence is a valuable trait for financial decision making and could eventually be used as a variable for selecting personnel. Mykytyn's study only compared novice and expert groups of financial decision makers with the finding that the experts, who had survived longer in the profession, were more field independent. The differences between the two groups could have been reflecting a change in cognitive style that results from many years on the job. The present results, in contrast, were predictive in nature, whereby a prior condition predicts future performance. The underlying skill that is represented here appears to be the ability to identify the really meaningful nuggets of information what could be a flood of superfluous information or information that is just "nice to know." This capability of cognitive processing would translate into a better use of the individual's cognitive channel capacity (Pascual-Leone 1970).

Gender effects were found for workload ratings, but not abilities or performance measures. The task was not physically demanding in the sense of heavy lifting, but it might have been so for some people because of the long time spent in a chair watching Powerpoint slides without a break and only making a simple but repetitive action. Gender effects in workload ratings have not been systematically reported in the past, and future research should consider whether a pattern across different types of tasks is taking shape. The best explanation for the findings come from Halpern et al. (2007) that the arithmetic-intensive task was less compatible with the interests of the females than it was for males; thus the TLX ratings reflected that the task was more demanding.

Finally, to tie up a couple loose ends, the psychosocial variables and the anagram test did not show any correlation with the TLX ratings or performance. Thus no data were reported for those variables. Those variables made a stronger contribution, however, in the assessment of *change* in the participants' optimizing and risk-taking tendencies as a function of increasing workload and fatigue as described in detail in the previous chapter.

References

Blanchette, I. (Ed.). (2014). *Emotion and reasoning*. New York: Psychology Press.

Boring, E. G. (1950). *History of experimental psychology* (2nd ed.). Englewood Cliffs: Prentice Hall.

Corr, P. J. (2010). Individual differences in cognition: In search of a general model of behavior control. In A. Gruszka, G. Matthews, & B. Szymura (Eds.), *Handbook of individual differences in cognition* (pp. 3–26). New York: Springer.

De Neys, W., & Osman, M. (Eds.). (2014). *New approaches in reasoning research*. New York: Psychology Press.

Gruszka, A., Matthews, G., & Szymura, B. (Eds.). (2010). *Handbook of individual differences in cognition* (pp. 3–26). New York: Springer.

Guastello, S. J., Shircel, A., Malon, M., & Timm, P. (2015). Individual differences in the experience of cognitive workload. *Theoretical Issues in Ergonomics Science, 16*, 20–52.

Halpern, D. F., Benbow, C. P., Geary, D. C., Gur, R. C., Hyde, J. S., & Gernsbacher, M. A. (2007). The science of sex differences in science and mathematics. *Psychological Science in the Public Interest, 8*(1), 1–51.

Karwowski, W. (2000). Symvatology: The science of an artifact-human compatibility. *Theoretical Issues in Ergonomics Science, 1*, 76–91.

Mykytyn, P. P., Jr. (1989). Group embedded figures test (GEFT): Individual differences, performance, and learning effects. *Educational and Psychological Measurement, 49*, 951–959.

NASA Ames Research Center (n.d.). *NASA Task Load Index (TLX) 1.0: Paper and pencil package*. Moffett Field: Author. Retrieved October 15, 2012, from http://humansystems.arc.nasa.gov/groups/TLX/paperpencil.html

Nygren, T. E. (1991). Psychometric properties of subjective workload measurement techniques: Implications for their use in the assessment of perceived mental workload. *Human Factors, 33*, 17–33.

Pascual-Leone, J. (1970). A mathematical model for the transition rule in Piaget's developmental stages. *Acta Psychologia, 32*, 301–345.

Warm, J. S., Parasuraman, R., & Matthews, G. (2008). Vigilance requires hard mental work and is stressful. *Human Factors, 50*, 433–441.

Wilhelms, E. A., & Reyna, V. F. (Eds.). (2015). *Neuroeconomics, judgment, and decision making*. New York: Psychology Press.

Chapter 5
The Performance-Variability Paradox: Optimizing

Stephen J. Guastello, Katherine Reiter, Anton Shircel, Paul Timm, Matthew Malon, and Megan Fabisch

Abstract The study presented in this chapter examined the relationship between performance variability and actual performance of financial decision makers who were working under experimental conditions of increasing workload and fatigue. The rescaled range statistic, also known as the Hurst exponent (H) was used as an index of variability. Although H is defined as having a range between 0 and 1, 45 % of the 172 time series generated by undergraduates were negative. Participants in the study chose the optimum investment out of sets of 3–5 options that were presented a series of 350 displays. The sets of options varied in both the complexity of the options and number of options under simultaneous consideration. Depending on experimental condition, participants to make their choices within 15 s or 7.5 s. Results showed that (a) negative H was possible and not a result of psychometric error; (b) negative H was associated with negative autocorrelations in a time series. (c) H was the best predictor of performance of the variables studied; (d) three other significant predictors were scores on an anagrams test and ratings of physical demands and performance demands; (e) persistence as evidenced by the autocorrelations was associated with ratings of greater time pressure. Furthermore, persistence and overall performance were correlated, "healthy" variability only exists

---

The majority of this chapter was previously published as a journal article with the permission of the Society for Chaos Theory in Psychology & Life Sciences. It has been edited for format: Guastello et al. (2014).

S.J. Guastello (✉) • K. Reiter
Marquette University, Milwaukee, WI, USA
e-mail: Stephen.guastello@marquette.edu

A. Shircel
Kohler Corporation, Sheboygan, WI, USA

P. Timm
Mayo Clinic, Rochester, MN, USA

M. Malon
Mount Mary University, Milwaukee, WI, USA

M. Fabisch
Illinois College of Optometry, Chicago, IL, USA

S.J. Guastello (ed.), *Cognitive Workload and Fatigue in Financial Decision Making*, Evolutionary Economics and Social Complexity Science 13,
DOI 10.1007/978-4-431-55312-0_5

within a limited range, and other individual differences related to ability and resistance to stress or fatigue are also involved in the prediction of performance.

5.1 Introduction

The study that is captured in this chapter reverts back to the nonlinear dynamics perspective (after a detour into linear statistics in Chap. 4), but this time the focus is on the individual time series of optimization data, the level of variability contained therein, and the further connection between variability and performance. The rescaled range statistic, also known as the Hurst exponent (H) was used as an index of variability. Although H is defined as having a range between 0 and $1, 45\,\%$ of the 172 time series generated negative values of H. Participants in the study chose the optimum investment out of sets of 3–5 options that were presented in a series of 350 displays. The sets of options also varied in their internal complexity. One experimental condition required participants to make their choices within 15 s, and the other condition required them to choose within 7.5 s. Results showed that (a) negative H was possible and not a result of psychometric error; (b) negative H was associated with negative autocorrelations in a time series. (c) H was the strongest of four predictors of performance; and (d) the persistence of the time series, as evidenced by the autocorrelations, was associated with ratings of greater time pressure. It can be concluded, furthermore, that persistence and overall performance were correlated, that "healthy" variability only exists within a limited range, and other individual differences related to ability and resistance to stress or fatigue are also involved in the prediction of performance.

5.2 The Paradox

There is a widespread supposition among human resources professionals that top performers are also *consistently* top performers. The same point has been made about investment fund specialists specifically (Amenc et al. 2004; Edwards and Caglayan 2001; Géhin 2003; Lowenstein 2006). Paradoxically, however, it is the residual variation in performance that actually facilitates adaptation and movement to new levels of performance (Mayer-Kress et al. 2009). The counterpoint between performance and variability is especially important because a substantial amount of within-person variability exists in the performance of virtually any task or job (Navarro et al. 2013). Thus the first objective of the present study was to examine the relationship between the variability of performance in an experimental financial decision making task and performance itself.

Entropy statistics have been useful for characterizing variability in numerous psychomotor, cognitive, and psychosocial functions (Guastello and Gregson 2011). Importantly, the variability has deterministic origins, and is not simply stochastic variability or random noise. Thus nonlinear metrics that preserve temporal patterns and arise from deterministic processes have become more useful than ordinary standard deviations for characterizing performance variability. The second objective of the present study, however, is to explore the possible uses of the Hurst exponent, H, as a measure of performance variability. H, also known as *rescaled range*, is a nonlinear metric that contrasts persistence, anti-persistence, and random walk modalities, and would thus appear to address the concerns of financial performance. In fact, H has been used relatively often to characterize the dynamics of time series of commodity prices and market indexes (Mandelbrot 1997; Peters 1991, 1994). What is new here is that the analysis is directed at series of decisions by *individuals*, rather than aggregate indexes or price charts produced by thousands of trading agents. Furthermore, the dynamics of cognitive workload and fatigue are likely to be prominent at the individual level, but not discernable in aggregate economic time series.

Although H is defined as having a range between 0 and 1, the analysis of the experimental data in this study produced extreme values of H that were very close to 0 and sometimes negative. To our knowledge the phenomenon of negative H values has only been reported in the literature once (Siad 2001), but it is possible that these "illegal" values occur more often. Thus the third objective of the study was to decipher the meaning of negative H, the nonlinear dynamics that it implies, and the properties of time series that make it likely to occur.

The fourth objective of the present study was to explain individual differences in variability patterns in terms of psychological variables that are currently being explored for their roles in cognitive workload and fatigue. The list includes cognitive abilities such as arithmetic, spelling, and field independent cognitive style; and psychosocial variables such as anxiety, PWE, conscientiousness, EI, and subjective ratings of workload. These variables might also explain individual differences in time series variability as captured by H because increases in the variability of performance are often associated with fatigue (Hong 2010).

5.2.1 *Healthy Variability*

Psychomotor functions such as walking display a substantial amount of variability in performance, such that it might not be possible to walking across the room exactly the same way twice. The current interpretation of this variability is that it serves to promote adaptation to walking surfaces, obstacle avoidance, and other environmental challenges. Healthy systems contain more variability than unhealthy systems; the latter tend toward rigidity and stereotypy (Bianciardi 2015; Correa et al. 2015; Guastello 2015; Guastello et al. 2013b; Harrison and Stergiou 2015; Katsavelis et al. 2010a, b; Kiefer and Myer 2015; Kurz et al. 2010; Morrison and Newell 2015; Navarro and Rueff-Lopes 2015; Pincus 2001; Stergiou and Decker 2011; Stergiou et al. 2006; Vargas et al. 2015). The rationale expanded from research on heart rate variability, which is again greater in normal electrocardiograms; overly periodic heart rates foretell an infarction (Cecen and Erkal 2009; Goldberger 1991; Goldberger et al. 1986). As a result of these findings, biomedical technologies seek to explore the origins of variability and hopefully restore it for patients who have become mobility-impaired due to stroke or other trauma. Psychologists guide clients and families toward greater flexibility in their coping strategies (Kato 2012; Pincus and Metten 2010).

In skill training, the residual level of variability in performance is intrinsic to developing new levels of skill (Mayer-Kress et al. 2009), which is thought to be not possible if the sources of variability did not exist. Discontinuities in performance can also be observed when skill advances to a new level or under conditions of workload and fatigue (Guastello 2014; Chaps. 2 and 3, this volume); the latter is usually, but not always, in a negative direction. The principles of *degrees of freedom* (Bernstein 1967; Marken 1991; Rosenbaum et al. 1991; Turvey 1990) and *minimum entropy* (Hong 2010) explain how the discontinuities in performance occur.

In any particular complex movement, each limb of the body is capable of moving in a limited number of ways, and the movements made by one limb restrict or facilitate movement by other limbs. The degrees of freedom are the number of component parts, such as muscles or neural networks that could function differently to produce the final performance result. A system of internally connected nodes of movement is more efficient than one in which all elements of movement are controlled by a central executive function. When a movement is being learned for the first time, several combinations of networks and movement are explored by the individual; once learning sets in, however, the movement combinations gravitate towards conserving degrees of freedom, which is in essence a path of least resistance. The gravitation process is essentially a self-organization dynamic. Cognitive behaviors are thought to emerge in more or less the same fashion with regard to the early and later stages of schematic development, the role of the executive functions of working memory, and the principle of conserving degrees of freedom (Guastello et al. 2013a; Hollis et al. 2009).

Automation in human-machine systems also produces a version of the performance-variability paradox (Bainbridge 1983; Sheridan 2002). Automation can produce high volumes of output with consistent quality and properties. By taking humans out of the proverbial loop, however, the machines cannot adapt to unusual circumstances; humans, which represent the cognitive executive function for the combined system, need to intervene. It appears that the greatest asset of automation is perhaps its greatest liability.

5.2.2 Minimum Entropy

The principle of *minimum entropy* (Hong 2010) describes the self-organizing phase shifts in performance. Given that there are multiple ways of performing or organizing a task, the approach that typically prevails is one that consumes the least amount of energy or exudes the least amount of entropy. Sometimes the agent needs to change to a different sequence of neural networks when one sequence has been subjected to an increased workload or fatigued. In situations involving increased workload, the modicum of flexibility produces "coping strategies" that serve the purpose of maintaining performance (Hancock and Warm 1989). Variability in performance increases under conditions of fatigue (as explained in Chap. 2), and it could be possible to restore performance levels by redistributing degrees of freedom. For instance, one might compensate for fatigue by slowing down the activity level thus reducing speed-related stress (Lorist and Faber 2011). Slowing down could help performance quality but not quantity; although this strategy may be sub-optimal it may be preferable based on the task's degrees of freedom and tolerance for error. The agent may also manipulate external factors involved in the task by reconfiguring the workspace or by making adjustments to the tools employed in the task; these represent the degrees of freedom inherent in the task itself.

Some recent studies offer some insights about the origins of the performance-variability paradox. In one (Guastello et al. 2013b), lower entropy in cognitive task performance was associated with fewer states of poor performance. The variability was confined to the higher levels of performance. In a study of motions that produce a serve in tennis, Bardy et al. (2013) found that the motions just proximal to the actual serve held very little variability, but the motions leading up to that point did contain substantial variability. The observation led to the interpretation that the actions that are most important to the end result vary very little, and the parts of the action that are less critical are free to vary. In other words, it does not always matter how one accomplishes the task so long as it is done well and on time.

A third insight came from a study of task switching, which was designed to externalize the cognitive processes that might be inherent in a complex task with, in this case, seven components (Guastello et al. 2012). Performance was better overall if there was less entropy in the ordering of the task components; this point was consistent with the minimum entropy principle. Not all participants in the study utilized the minimum entropy principle, however; some exhibited coherent strategies that changed over the course of the experiment period, and others exhibited a random strategy throughout the time series.

Task switching, when it is under complete control of the experimenter or an automated system produces a demand on the executive function of working memory that is usually observed in response delays (Andreadis and Quinlan 2010; Rubinstein et al. 2001) and performance decrements associated with fatigue. When it is under the control of the individual operator, however, it can *alleviate* fatigue effects (Guastello et al. 2013a; Hancock 2007). The latter reflects the redistribution response that occurs when the minimum entropy principle encounters fatigue.

5.3 Rescaled Range Analysis

5.3.1 Properties of H

A time series variable, X with T observations is broken into several subseries of length n; n is arbitrary, but $n = pT$ (integer portion) is recommended (Sprott and Rowlands 2003). Then for each subseries, the grand mean is subtracted from X, and the differences summed:

$$Y_n = \sum_{i=1}^{n} (X_i - <X>) \tag{5.1}$$

The range, R, is the difference between the maximum and minimum values of Y_n. Then,

$$R/s = (\pi n/2)^H \tag{5.2}$$

where σ is the standard deviation of the entire series; $0 < H < 1$ (Sprott 2003, p. 225). Actual values of H may vary somewhat due to the choice of n and the time scale represented by the individual observations.

H has some useful properties. A value of 0.5 represents *Brownian motion*, meaning that the deflections in a time series can be upward or downward with equal probability on each step. Brownian motion has a Gaussian distribution and is non-stationary. Values that diverge from 0.5 in either direction are non-Markovian, meaning that there is memory in the system beyond the first step prior to an observation (Mandelbrot 1997, p. 160).

$H > 0.5$ denotes *persistence*. Deflections in a time series gravitate toward a fixed point if they are high enough. For instance the volumes of water flowing through some of the major rivers in the world are fairly steady over many years (Hurst 1951; Mandelbrot 1983). The autocorrelation of observations in a time series is positive. The relationship between H and the lag-1 autocorrelation, r, is:

$$r = 2^{(2H-1)} - 1 \tag{5.3}$$

(Weisstein 1999, pp. 1102–1103).

Values in the neighborhood of 0.75 represent pink noise or self-organizing systems. They have power law distributions with negative shape parameters (Mandelbrot 1983, 1997), thus suggesting a relationship between H and the fractal dimension (Mandelbrot 1975), which is:

$$D_F = 2 - H. \tag{5.4}$$

The caveat is that the relationship holds for self-similar fractals and graphs that are projected deliberately onto a two-dimensional space. Those structures have unique fractal (box-counting) dimensions. For multi-fractal structures that are projected onto a two-dimensional graph and which characterize many economic time series,

$$D_M = 1/H \tag{5.5}$$

(Mandelbrot 1997). Note that D_M becomes remarkably high as $H \to 0$.

$H < 0.5$ denotes *anti-persistence*. Deflections in a time series are self-avoiding such as one might observe in an oscillation. The autocorrelation of observations in a time series should be negative.

5.3.2 *Negative Values of* H

The time series of interest in the present study involve $H \to 0$, based on a sneak-peak at the data as it was being analyzed. In fact some of the obtained values of H ranged between 0 and −0.05. On the one hand, calculated values so close to 0.0 could result from statistical error sources. If those sources of error are ruled out, the known boundaries of $0 < H < 1$ would still apply as usual.

On the other hand, it is possible to calculate H for some chaotic attractors and obtain negative values of H. Data sets from Sprott and Rowlands (2003) for the Lozi Map ($N = 2000$), Ikeda attractor ($N = 2000$), and Henon attractor ($N = 2000$) show $H = -0.0527$, −0.0472, and −0.0367 respectively. Those series are fully deterministic, meaning that measurement error does not exist. The time series appears long enough to cover the full range of dynamics so that the segmentation that is performed on the time series when calculating H is not based on an overly short times series. The Lozi, Ikeda, and Henon attractors have attractor dimensions were calculated as 1.398, 1.662, and 1.239, which is not the same as the calculation of the D_F and D_M for a time series expressed in Eqs. 5.4 and 5.5.

Tentatively, therefore, negative values of H can possibly exist. If $H < 0$ were plugged into Eq. 5.3, a strong negative autocorrelation would be produced. Thus it would be advisable to calculate the lag-1 autocorrelation to determine if there is any consistency between low-H and negative autocorrelation. If $H < 0$ were plugged into Eq. 5.4, $D_F > 2$ would be obtained; this result would make sense if the series were interpretable as arising from a control parameter that adds a small amount of a third dimension to the graph of the time series.

Although negative fractal dimensions are not routinely associated with economic time series, they do show up in Mandelbrot's (1983) analyses of landscapes. Positive dimensions are associated with rugged mountains and valley between them that all sit above the flat plane of the terrain. Negative values are associated with chasms and canyons that drop below the flat plane of the terrain. A negative H was reported for an economic time series nonetheless. Siad (2001) analyzed a series of market indexes for the Thailand stock exchange that contained a sharp increase followed by a sharp decrease. Analyses showed mixed results in that the largest

Lyapunov exponent was positive, signifying the potential for chaos, the BDS statistic was not significant, signifying no nonlinear events, and H was slightly negative. Said interpreted the negative H as denoting a "black hole" of some sort.

The next question is whether anything akin to a canyon or a black hole could exist in an economic time series. Most of the time series in Said's graph looked plausibly chaotic with relatively steady boundaries, but the sharp upward and downward movements that he was trying to explain bore a closer resemblance to a speculative bubble. Speculative bubbles are characteristic of cusp catastrophe dynamics (Guastello 1995; Rosser 1997), which contain a repellor between the two stable states in the high-bifurcation side of the response surface. Later researchers (Ahmed et al. 2010), however, discerned that a speculative bubble was occurring in the Thailand stock exchange (1991–2006) and in many other emerging markets during the same time period, and that the BDS statistic for the Thailand stock exchange data was indeed significant. The BDS statistics identifies the presence of dependent errors in a time series that are produced by an underlying nonlinear process; it does not identify *which* nonlinear process is operating, however. The connection between bifurcations, repellors, and negative H warrants further investigation, however.

5.3.3 Statistical Significance of H

The Chow F test is sometimes used to determine whether H differs significantly from 0.5. The test compares variances on the segments of the time series of observations used to produce H. Segments can be defined in other ways, such as before, during, and after an apparent speculative bubble (Ahmed et al. 2006; Ahmed et al. 2010). F can also be computed using both the slope and intercepts of the local autoregression or using the slope only. Rejecting the null hypothesis would indicate that a process other than a random walk is operating, whereby variances were not homogenous across segments.

The logic of the test, however, does not appear to consider that when extreme values of H are operating, H would also have consistent variances. Autocorrelations close to 1.0 can be produced when values were the same across the entire time series, as one might obtain from a fixed point. Autocorrelations very close to 0.0 can be produced when a perfect oscillator is operating, which would also produce homogenous variances across segments. Thus the test would not help with the present problem of discerning whether negative values of H are the result of error variance.

The present problem, however, offered some advantages associated with taking data from a sample of human participants, all of whom were subjected to systematic exposure, rather than single economic time series, such as summary indices from a stock market that would all be assessed individually. The mean of the sample of H values can be tested using a one-sample t-test against the population value of 0; the 95 % confidence interval would not include 0.0 if the sample mean was negative. Standard errors of the mean would reflect variance due to sampling, psychometric, or other sources of error variance.

Another advantage of the large sample strategy is that it becomes possible to assess psychometric error specifically and determine whether a *confidence interval around a particular value* of H does not include $H = 0$ in its range. The reliability of a (mental) test score is the ratio of true score variance to total score variance, calculated over all the test items; in the present case, the 70 observations in the individuals' time series constitute the 70 items on the "test." Of the various measures of reliability that have been developed over the last century, Cronbach's alpha is perhaps the most widely used and the most pertinent to the present problem:

$$\alpha = (n/n - 1)\sqrt{\left(\sigma_T^2 - \sum \sigma_i^2\right)/\sigma_T^2} \tag{5.6}$$

where $n =$ number of test items, σ_T^2 is the total score variance, and σ_i^2 is the variance of a test item that is summed over all items. α is based on the principle that all items should be correlated with the total test score if in fact all items are drawn from the same "universe" of items that could measure a construct; see Lord and Novick (1968) for the derivation and further commentary. If it can be assumed that the reliability of H is directly tied to the reliability of the 70-item time series, and not attenuated by the calculations that produced H from the original series of observations of performance, the standard error of measurement is

$$SEM_H = \sigma_H \sqrt{(1 - \alpha)}. \tag{5.7}$$

The 95 % confidence interval is thus

$$H \pm \left[t_{(df=120)} {*} SEM_H\right] \tag{5.8}$$

5.4 Hypotheses

The hypotheses were organized around the four questions addressed by the study: (a) Is there an association between performance level and performance variability? (b) Can H be used as a viable indicator of the performance variability and persistence in this context? (c) Are negative values of H possible and interpretable? (d) Can performance variability be explained by cognitive abilities, psychosocial variables, or subjective ratings of workload?

The first three hypotheses were tested using a conventional repeated ANOVA experimental design: There should be an effect for differences in workload, speed or time pressure, and the interaction between the two main effects. The conventional lens would provide a basis for interpreting the nonlinear dynamics that were involved in the next four hypotheses.

The fourth hypothesis was that H can be negative, contrary to the prevailing theory. The strategy here was to compare the sample mean with a target value of 0.0

and to assess the standard errors of measurement associated with extreme scores, as defined in Eqs. 5.6, 5.7, and 5.8.

The fifth hypothesis was that H would be correlated with the autocorrelation of the time series as expected from theoretical relationships. This hypothesis was tested for the lag-1 autocorrelation, the optimal autocorrelation, and the lag of the optimal autocorrelation. It was anticipated that the effect size for the relationship could be compromised by the restriction of range of value of H or the autocorrelations in the sample, however.

The sixth hypothesis was that there should be a correlation between H and overall performance such that more persistent performance would be associated with better performance overall.

The seventh hypothesis was that H could be explained by individual differences in cognitive abilities, psychosocial variables, and subjective ratings of workload that were introduced in previous chapters and incorporated in the cusp catastrophe models of cognitive workload and fatigue for the financial decision making task.

The eighth hypothesis was an outgrowth of the fifth, when bimodal distributions were discovered for the optimal autocorrelations and optimal lags within the sample. The hypothesis was that the experimental manipulation for time pressure would be responsible, at least in part, for individual differences in H, lag-1 autocorrelations, optimal autocorrelations, and optimal lags. The rationale is that time pressure on the decisions could have an impact on the temporal dynamics of the performance time series.

5.5 Method

The experimental procedure, participants, and measurements were described in Chap. 3. The participants for this segment were the 172 individuals who were assigned to experimental conditions in which they completed the series of 350 stimuli. Participants were randomly assigned to one of two speed conditions: 15 s per item ($n = 102$), and 7.5 s per item ($n = 69$). The faster condition was introduced to the experimental protocol after about 30 data sets in the slower condition were collected. Thus the two subsamples are of unequal size. The experimental sessions lasted 2.5 h and accommodated small groups of up to 10 participants each.

Participants started with 5-min timed tests of arithmetic and spelling abilities, and an untimed survey instrument measuring anxiety, conscientiousness, PWE, and EI. The GEFT and the mixed anagram test followed the survey.

For the analyses involving H, autocorrelations, and regression analyses, the full time series of 350 items was aggregated into 70 packets of 5 items, with a score ranging from 1 to 5 on each packet. No correction for guessing was applied. The time series of 70 packets was then used for the analyses using the Chaos Data Analyzer (Sprott and Rowlands 2003).

5.6 Results

5.6.1 Distribution of H

The H values for the 172 participants ranged from −0.13 to 0.29 (M = −0.003, SD = 0.049, standard error of the mean (SE) = 0.004); 43 % of the H values were negative. Four examples of performance time series appear in Fig. 5.1, two of which have positive but near-zero values of H, and two produced negative values of H. The trend line in the figures was produced by the Chaos Data Analyzer (Sprott and Rowlands 2003) as an extrapolation of a trend formed by the difference between performance at the first observation, and performance at the $\sqrt{N}^{th}$ observation. Deflections in performance during the first five blocks of trials in which the complexity of the options was gradually increased appear left of the center line. Observations to the right of the centerline were produced in the second half of the time series in which the items and options within items were randomized. There was a substantial hysteresis effect observed toward the end of the series.

The one-sample t-test showed that the mean H was not significantly different from 0. The 95 % confidence interval around the mean was $-0.010 < M < 0.004$. The conclusion about the dynamics was that the time series were strongly antipersistent to the limit of H.

The α reliability of the 70-item performance series was 0.85. The calculation of α on the first 50 packets was 0.80. Thus it would be fair to conclude that the volatility of the last observations in the series resulted from a deterministic process and not from measurement error. The SEM was calculated using α = 0.85. The upper bound of the 95 % confidence interval around the lowest value of H was $H + \left[t_{(df=120)} * SEM_H\right] = -.128 + .038 = -.09$. Furthermore, 16.4 % of the sample produced values of H with upper bounds of their confidence intervals falling below 0.0. Thus the observed negative values of H are *not* the result of measurement error and need to be explained another way.

The lag-1 autocorrelations ranged from −0.37 to 0.61 (M = 0.030, SD = 0.165, SE = 0.013). The autocorrelations based on optimal lags also ranged from −0.37 to 0.61 (M = 0.080, SD = 0.242, SE = 0.019). The lag length for the optimal autocorrelations ranged from 1 to 16 (M = 6.56, SD = 5.14, SE = 0.393).

The distributions of the four statistics appear in Fig. 5.2. H and lag-1 autocorrelations showed a normal-appearing distribution. Optimal autoregression values were distributed bimodally with modes at −0.25 and 0.25. This result suggested that the participants adopted two different strategies; one strategy favored persistence throughout the series of stimuli, and the other favored anti-persistence in the form of an oscillating strategy. The distribution of optimal lag length was irregular, but the histogram suggested bimodality such that the local modes for optimal lags were 2 and 16.

An important relationship here is the connection between negative H and the direction of the autocorrelation functions. The distribution of H was dichotomized between positive and negative values, as was the lag-1 autocorrelation; the

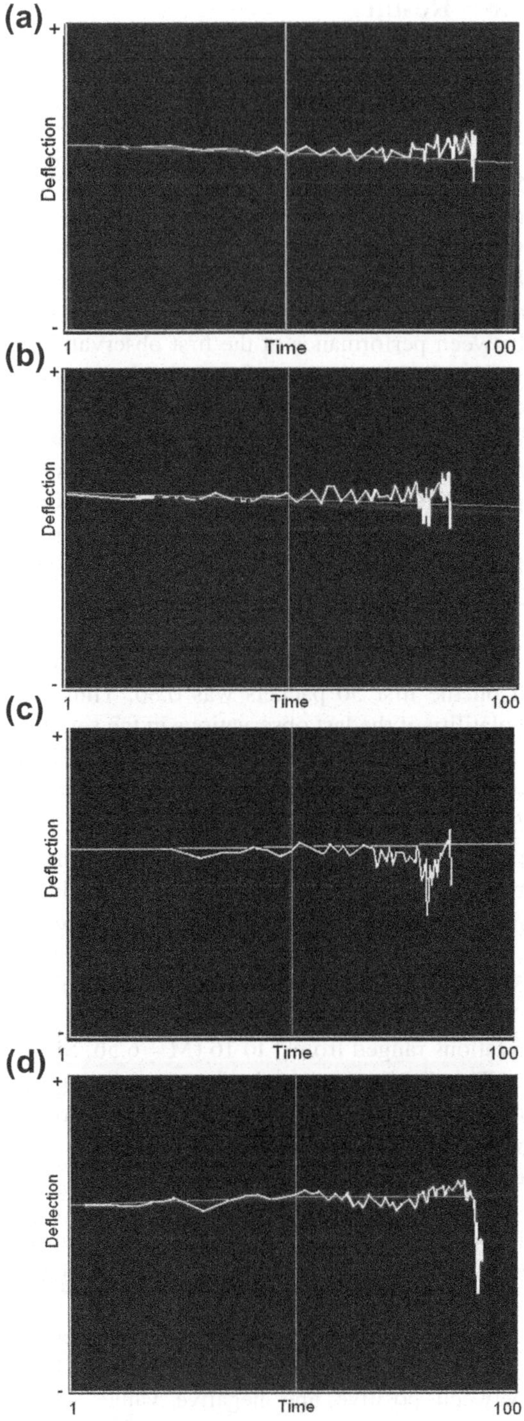

Fig. 5.1 Four examples of rescaled range times series for optimizing: (**a**) $H = -0.0431$, (**b**) $H = -0.0870$, (**c**) $H = +0.0155$, (**d**) $H = +0.0362$ (After Guastello et al. (2014) with permission of Society for Chaos Theory in Psychology & Life Sciences)

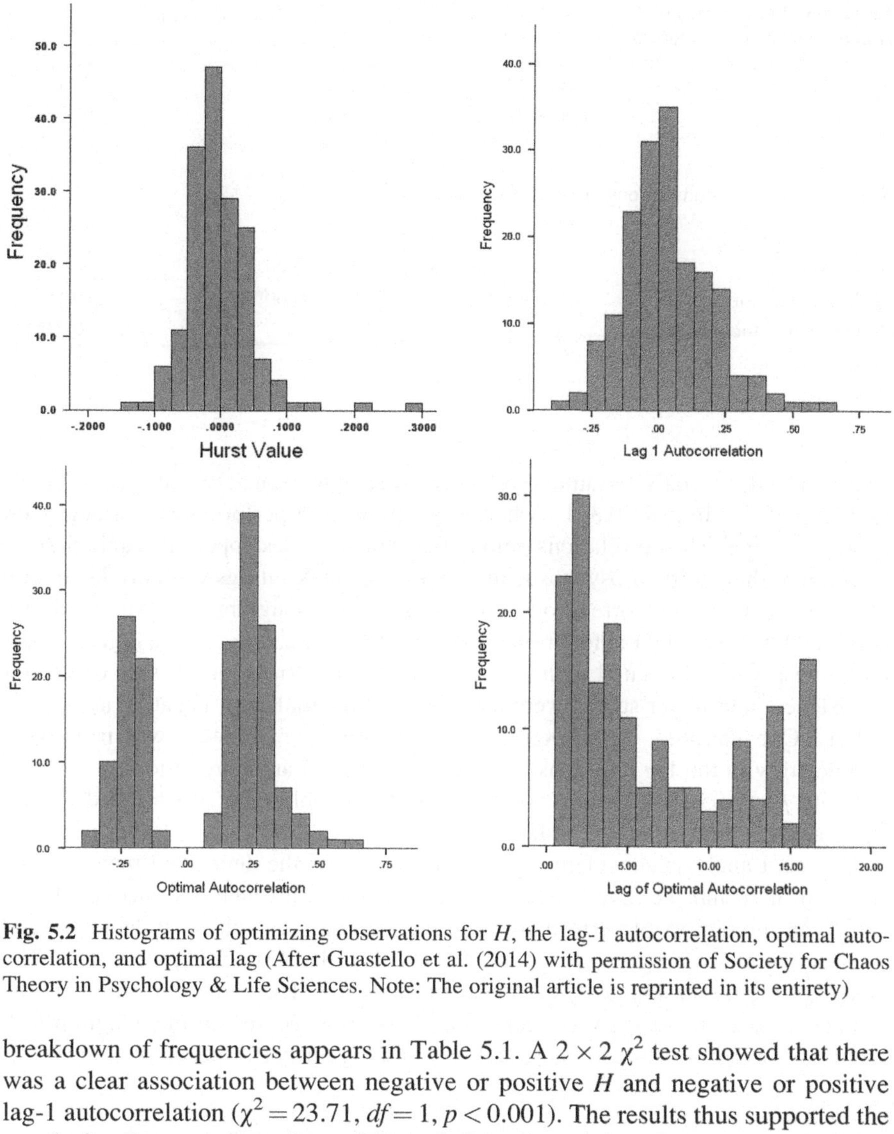

Fig. 5.2 Histograms of optimizing observations for *H*, the lag-1 autocorrelation, optimal autocorrelation, and optimal lag (After Guastello et al. (2014) with permission of Society for Chaos Theory in Psychology & Life Sciences. Note: The original article is reprinted in its entirety)

breakdown of frequencies appears in Table 5.1. A 2×2 χ^2 test showed that there was a clear association between negative or positive *H* and negative or positive lag-1 autocorrelation ($\chi^2 = 23.71$, $df = 1$, $p < 0.001$). The results thus supported the conclusion that negative values of *H* result from time series of observations that are negatively autocorrelated.

5.6.2 *Regression Analyses*

The next phase of the investigation sought connections between *H* and the autocorrelations with variables that were thought to explain workload and fatigue

Table 5.1 Frequencies of H and Lag-1 autocorrelations

	Lag-1 autocorrelation	
	Negative	Positive
H negative	51	32
H positive	22	67

Table 5.2 Correlations among structural variables

	2	3	4
1. Hurst	0.46***	0.20	−0.14
2. Lag-1 autocorrelation		0.60***	−0.15
3. Optimal autocorrelation			−0.27***
4. Optimal lag			

***$p < 0.001$, all other correlations are NS

effects. For these analyses, autocorrelations were transformed by their natural logs, such that $r'_{PP} = \ln(r_{PP} + 0.371)$, where r_{PP} denotes the performance variable with itself over time. The correlations among the four statistics appear in Table 5.2.

None of the ability or psychosocial variables or TLX ratings was correlated with H or the optimal autocorrelation. One variable, the anagram test, was modestly correlated with the lag-1 autocorrelation ($r = 0.18$, $t = 2.20$, $p < 0.05$); higher scores on the test were associated with larger positive autocorrelations, a sign of greater persistence, and lower scores were associated with smaller or negative autocorrelations. One variable, the TLX rating of performance pressure, was negatively correlated with the lag length associated with optimal autocorrelation ($r = -0.17$, $t = 2.30$, $p < 0.05$); lag lengths were shorter for people who experienced greater performance pressure on the task.

The next analysis considered total performance as the dependent measure as a function of H and the other research variables. Stepwise analysis uncovered four significant predictors of performance: H, the anagram test, physical demands, and TLX performance pressure ($R = 0.37$, $R^2 = 0.14$, $F(4, 143) = 5.60$, $p < 0.001$). The details of the regression analysis appear in Table 5.3. The better performers in the sample were more strongly antipersistent, had lower scores on the anagram test, reported lower physical demands, and reported higher performance pressure.

5.6.3 *Time Pressure and Temporal Dynamics*

Mean differences in H, lag-1 autocorrelations, optimal autocorrelations, and optimal lags were compared for the faster-speed and slower-speed groups using independent samples t-tests, where equal variances were not assumed, and the natural log transformation was retained for the autocorrelations. The differences in the mean optimal autocorrelation were significant ($t = -2.05$, $df = 165.04$, $p < 0.05$).

Table 5.3 Multiple regression predicting total performance

	β	t	r	R^2
Hurst	−0.21	−2.73***	−0.23***	0.05
Anagrams	−0.15	−1.87*	−0.16**	0.08
Physical demands	−0.17	−2.18**	−0.19**	0.11
Performance demands	0.17	2.14**	0.18**	0.14

$^{*}p<0.10$, $^{**}p<0.05$, $^{***}p<0.01$

The average autocorrelations were 0.05 in the slower condition (SD = 0.26), and 0.12 in the faster condition (SD = 0.22).

The differences in the mean optimal lag were also significant ($t = 2.06$, $df = 156.41$, $p < 0.05$). The average optimal lag was longer for the slower conditions (M = 7.21, SD = 5.31) compared to the faster condition (M = 5.61, SD = 4.75). No significant differences were obtained for H or the lag-1 autocorrelation as a function of speed.

5.7 Discussion

The results of the study provided some new insights regarding the nature of H and its relationship to performance in financial decision making. The dynamics associated with values of H offered some further insights regarding the underlying cognitive processes associated with workload and fatigue effects.

5.7.1 Persistence and Antipersistence

The mean H for this task was −0.003, which was not significantly different from 0.0. The interpretation was that the dynamics of decision making in this experimental context was strongly antipersistent in the extreme of H, implying an oscillating function. The lag-1 autocorrelations were negative for 42 % of the sample, which also denotes oscillation. The other 58 % were more consistent in their performance overall. The graphs showed undampening as the experiment progressed, so the strength of the oscillations was a matter of degree for both within-person trends and across people.

Although H was constructed as a metric ranging from 0 to 1, the range of values has its exceptions based on the results of this study. It now appears that small negative values of H are possible. One third of the negative values could not be attributed to measurement error, however, and they are associated with negative lag-1 autocorrelations within the time series of performance. Negative autocorrelations also suggest an oscillating function. Three of the prototype interpretations of H – persistent, self-organizing pink noise, and random walks – characterize types of variations around a steady state. Steady states are most akin to fixed point attractors and would imply positive autocorrelations. Antipersistence, however, could involve a limit cycle, dampened or undampened oscillators, hysteresis around a repellor, or one of a few types of chaotic functions. The more complex dynamics, such as those involving bifurcation functions, could be more likely to produce negative values of *H*.

Arguably, (un)dampened oscillators fall outside the intended use of *H*. It is also possible that different algorithms that use different strategies for making the segments that contribute to *H*, or the local variances, could produce different results. Clearly more work is needed in this area.

By the same token, the relationship between the sign of *H* and the sign of the lag-1 autocorrelation was not perfect; the χ^2 value converts to a ϕ coefficient (interpret as a product–moment correlation) of 0.37. The attenuated relationship between the two metrics could be related to the finding that the lag-1 autocorrelation was not always the optimal autocorrelation. Optimal correlations were found most often at lag 2 in this experiment, with an average optimal lag length between 6 and 7.

The attenuated relationship could also have resulted from restrictions of range on both variables. Further research could investigate wider ranges. The challenge, however, would be to find a task or compatible tasks that could produce the full range of dynamics.

5.7.2 The Performance-Variability Paradox

Initially, the paradox required the resolution of two propositions: (a) The best performers are the most consistent performers. (b) A modicum of variability is necessary to attain the highest levels of performance. Concomitant to (a), the system gravitates toward minimizing entropy in performance (Guastello et al. 2012, 2013b; Hong 2010). The tentative resolution was that both propositions could be true if the individual spends less time in the lowest performance regions and only varies within the relatively good regions (Guastello et al. 2013b). The plot now seems to be thickening such that (c) antipersistence is associated with better performance under some circumstances.

Proposition (c) was uncovered by shifting the metric of deterministic variability from an entropy-based calculation (in the task switching studies and most of the studies on optimal variability mentioned at the beginning of the chapter) to *H*. The type of persistence usually associated with the best performers would be that of $H > 0.5$, and a contrast against the random walk interpretation of performance. Antipersistence is actually no more random in that sense than a black-noise steady state. If one were to characterize a perfectly repeating set of states as an intact symbolic string, the entropy of that string relative to other events that creep in would be very low. It was already shown, however, that Shannon entropy and topological entropy would treat that string differently. Shannon entropy would assign a relatively higher value depending on the number of states that existed within the string, whereas topological entropy would not because it treats patterns of elementary states as single states. Thus the metric of deterministic variability contributes its own idiosyncrasies of interpretation.

Some other interesting findings concerning the human side of performance variability were uncovered. Performance was better if the perceived performance pressure was greater. That connection seems straightforward. Unexpectedly, however, performance pressure was associated with shorter lag length in the optimal autocorrelations. Memory in the system was becoming shorter, although the time series remained non-Markovian in most cases. The shorter lag functions could have been associated with participants who consolidated their cognitive strategies more quickly than others with longer lag lengths; this point should be pursued further in future research.

The better performers also scored lower on the anagrams test. This result makes sense because anagrams require divergent thinking, and the task required the repeated use of an arithmetic schema, which would be a convergent operation. Attempts to use divergent thinking (or think creatively) might have interfered with the consistent use of the calculation schemata. It was also noteworthy, however, that the arithmetic test scores were not correlated with optimizing performance. The roles of divergent thinking and arithmetic ability in the dynamics of cognitive workload and fatigue were investigated in Chap. 3.

The better performers gave the task lower ratings for performance demands. The physical demands of watching a PowerPoint presentation and making mental calculations are rather low overall, compared to the efforts of steel workers or urban emergency response teams. The individual differences in ratings should be interpreted accordingly as being highly relative to the college students' lives. The connection between higher ratings of physical demands in a low-demand situation could be indicative of an emotional response, perhaps something akin to a psychosomatic response in some circumstances (Guastello et al. 2015). An alternative view was also offered in the previous chapter that sitting in a chair making responses to a Powerpoint for this 2 h task could be more physically uncomfortable than what was previously imagined.

5.7.3 Cognitive Workload and Fatigue

Studies in nonlinear dynamics support the notion that variability in performance over time is fairly widespread across people and jobs. Performance can be discontinuous, falling into a different attractor state as a result of cognitive workload and fatigue. Cognitive workload and fatigue effects are two separate processes that occur simultaneously along with other conditions that improve performance over time. The present study examined finer-grained changes in performance over time under conditions in which workload and fatigue effects were both operating along with any other compensatory effects. The new insight is that performance over time was strongly antipersistent, as if something were oscillating. The same effect would arise from hysteresis around a repellor, which is likely the case in the cusp catastrophe models of workload and fatigue.

The oscillations grew larger as the experiment progressed. The deviations from the underlying trend were smaller in the first five blocks of trials in which the problems had a fixed level of complexity throughout each block. The deviations increased in the second half of the series in which the items were randomized. One might have guessed that the oscillations in performance that were occurring between single items would be flattened out by using packets of five items as the performance observation; that was apparently not the case. The time series usually concluded with very strong oscillations that are usually associated with fatigue.

One psychological question is now, "What caused the sudden increase in variability during the random item segment of the task?" A probable answer is that the participants were experiencing task switching costs during the random phase. Although the task involved was the same for all items in most respects, the use of simple or extended mental calculation models on an unpredictable basis could have been responsible for the increase in variability that would lead to fatigue in the end.

Another psychological question is to assess how the behavior of the students in the study compares with that of professional fund managers. So far, there is only limited data showing that professionals tend to be more field independent (Mykytyn 1989), but that variable was not unique in the regression analysis of individual differences here. Conceivably oscillations could be produced by managers who are trading off one or another fund criterion in successive decisions, perhaps in order to achieve a desired portfolio balance. The present experiment did not include portfolio constraints or other types of serially dependent dynamic decisions, however.

Finally, the bimodality observed for the distribution of optimal lag autocorrelations and optimal lag length requires some further mathematical modeling and psychological study. The presence of oscillations does not necessarily support the presence of hysteresis around a catastrophe manifold, but they could result from hysteresis rather than a limit cycle. A related mystery is the role of time pressure on the optimal autoregression and optimal lag. There now seems to be a cognitive dynamic occurring that has not been explored yet in the stress and performance literature. The usual questions – who, what, when, why, and how – are good places to start.

References

Ahmed, E., Li, H., & Rosser, J. B., Jr. (2006). Nonlinear bubbles in Chinese stock markets in the 1990s. *Eastern Economic Journal, 40*, 1–18.

Ahmed, E., Rosser, J. B., Jr., & Uppal, J. Y. (2010). Emerging markets and stock market bubbles: Nonlinear speculation? *Emerging Markets and Trade, 46*(4), 23–40.

Amenc, N., Curtis, S., & Martellini, L. (2004). *The alpha and omega of hedge fund performance measurement*. Lille: EDHEC Risk and Asset Management Research Centre. Retrieved

December 15, 2011, from http://www.edhecrisk.com/performance_and_style_analysis/Hendge_funds_performance

Andreadis, N., & Quinlan, P. T. (2010). Task switching under predictable and unpredictable circumstances. *Attention, Perception, and Psychophysics, 72*, 1776–1790.

Bainbridge, L. (1983). Ironies of automation. *Automatica, 19*, 775–779.

Bardy, B. G., Lagarde, J., & Mottet, D. (2013). Dynamics of skill acquisition in multimodal technological environments. In M. Bergamasco, B. Bardy, & D. Gopher (Eds.), *Skill training in multimodal virtual environments* (pp. 31–45). Boca Raton: CRC Press.

Bernstein, N. (1967). *The coordination and regulation of movements*. Oxford: Pergamon.

Bianciardi, G. (2015). Differential diagnosis: Shape and function, fractal tools in the pathology lab. *Nonlinear Dynamics, Psychology, & Life Sciences, 19*, 437–464.

Cecen, A. A., & Erkal, C. (2009). The long march: From monofractals to endogenous multifractality in heart rate variability analysis. *Nonlinear Dynamics, Psychology, and Life Science, 13*, 181–206.

Correa, U. C., Benda, R. N., de Oliveira, D. L., Uginowitsch, H., Freudenheim, A. M., & Tani, G. (2015). Different faces of variability in the adaptive process of motor skill learning. *Nonlinear Dynamics, & Life Sciences, 19*, 465–488.

Edwards, F. R., & Caglayan, M. O. (2001). Hedge fund performance and manager skill. *Journal of Futures Markets, 21*, 1003–1028.

Géhin, W. (2003). *Hedge fund performance*. Lille: EDHEC Risk and Asset Management Research Centre. Retrieved December 15, 2011, from http://www.edhec-risk.com/performance_and_style_analysis/Hendge_funds_performance

Goldberger, A. L. (1991). Is normal behavior chaotic or homeostatic? *News in Physiological Science, 6*, 87–91.

Goldberger, A. L., Bhargava, V., West, B. J., & Mandell, A. J. (1986). Some observations on the question: Is ventricular fibrillation chaos? *Physica D, 19*, 282–289.

Guastello, S. J. (1995). *Chaos, catastrophe, and human affairs: Applications of nonlinear dynamics to work, organizations, and social evolution*. Hillsdale: Lawrence Erlbaum Associates.

Guastello, S. J. (2014). Catastrophe models for cognitive workload and fatigue: Memory functions, multitasking, vigilance, financial decisions and risk. *Proceedings of the Human Factors and Ergonomics Society, 58*, 908–912.

Guastello, S. J. (2015). The complexity of the psychological self and the principle of optimum variability. *Nonlinear Dynamics, Psychology, & Life Sciences, 19*, 511–528.

Guastello, S. J., & Gregson, R. A. M. (Eds.). (2011). *Nonlinear dynamical systems analysis for the behavioral sciences using real data*. Boca Raton: CRC Press/Taylor & Francis.

Guastello, S. J., Gorin, H., Huschen, S., Peters, N. E., Fabisch, M., & Poston, K. (2012). New paradigm for task switching strategies while performing multiple tasks: Entropy and symbolic dynamics analysis of voluntary patterns. *Nonlinear Dynamics, Psychology, and Life Sciences, 16*, 471–497.

Guastello, S. J., Boeh, H., Gorin, H., Huschen, S., Peters, N. E., Fabisch, M., & Poston, K. (2013a). Cusp catastrophe models for cognitive workload and fatigue: A comparison of seven task types. *Nonlinear Dynamics, Psychology, and Life Sciences, 17*, 23–47.

Guastello, S. J., Gorin, H., Huschen, S., Peters, N. E., Fabisch, M., Poston, K., & Weinberger, K. (2013b). The minimum entropy principle and task performance. *Nonlinear Dynamics, Psychology, and Life Sciences, 17*, 405–424.

Guastello, S. J., Reiter, K., Shircel, A., Timm, P., Malon, M., & Fabisch, M. (2014). The performance-variability paradox, financial decision making, and the curious case of negative Hurst exponents. *Nonlinear Dynamics, Psychology, and Life Sciences, 18*, 297–328.

Guastello, S. J., Shircel, A., Malon, M., & Timm, P. (2015). Individual differences in the experience of cognitive workload. *Theoretical Issues in Ergonomics Science, 16*(1), 20–52.

Hancock, P. A. (2007). On the process of automation transition in multitask human-machine systems. *IEEE Transactions on Systems, Man, and Cybernetics - Part A: Systems and Humans, 37*, 586–598.

Hancock, P. A., & Warm, J. S. (1989). A dynamic model of stress and sustained attention. *Human Factors, 31*, 519–537.
Harrison, S. J., & Stergiou, N. (2015). Complex adaptive behavior in dexterous action. *Nonlinear Dynamics, Psychology, & Life Sciences, 19*, 345–394.
Hollis, G., Kloos, H., & Van Orden, G. C. (2009). Origins of order in cognitive activity. In S. J. Guastello, M. Koopmans, & D. Pincus (Eds.), *Chaos and complexity in psychology: The theory of nonlinear dynamical systems* (pp. 206–242). New York: Cambridge University Press.
Hong, S. L. (2010). The entropy conservation principle: Applications in ergonomics and human factors. *Nonlinear Dynamics, Psychology, and Life Sciences, 14*, 291–315.
Hurst, H. E. (1951). Long-term storage capacity of reservoirs. *Transactions of the American Society of Civil Engineers, 116*, 770–808.
Kato, T. (2012). Development of the Coping Flexibility Scale: Evidence for the coping flexibility hypothesis. *Journal of Counseling Psychology, 59*, 262–273.
Katsavelis, D., Muhkerjee, M., Decker, L., & Stergiou, N. (2010a). Variability of lower extremity joint kinematics during backward walking in a virtual environment. *Nonlinear Dynamics, Psychology, and Life Sciences, 14*, 165–178.
Katsavelis, D., Muhkerjee, M., Decker, L., & Stergiou, N. (2010b). The effect of virtual reality on gait variability. *Nonlinear Dynamics, Psychology, and Life Sciences, 14*, 239–256.
Kiefer, A. W., & Myer, G. D. (2015). Training the antifragile athlete: A preliminary analysis of neuromuscular training effects on muscle activation dynamics. *Nonlinear Dynamics, Psychology, & Life Sciences, 19*, 489–511.
Kurz, M. J., Markopoulou, K., & Stergiou, N. (2010). Attractor divergence as a metric for assessing walking balance. *Nonlinear Dynamics, Psychology, and Life Sciences, 14*, 151–164.
Lord, F. M., & Novick, M. R. (1968). *Statistical theories of mental test scores*. Reading: Addison-Wesley.
Lorist, M. M., & Faber, L. G. (2011). Consideration of the influence of mental fatigue on controlled and automatic cognitive processes. In P. Ackerman (Ed.), *Cognitive fatigue* (pp. 105–126). Washington, DC: American Psychological Association.
Lowenstein, L. (2006). Search for rational investors in a perfect storm: A behavioral perspective. *The Journal of Behavioral Finance, 7*, 66–74.
Mandelbrot, B. B. (1975). Stochastic models for the Earth's relief, the shape and the fractal dimension of the coastlines, and the number-area rule for islands. *Proceedings of the National Academy of Sciences, USA, 72*, 3825–3828.
Mandelbrot, B. B. (1983). *The fractal geometry of nature*. New York: Freeman.
Mandelbrot, B. B. (1997). *Fractals and scaling in finance: Discontinuity, concentration and risk*. New York: Springer.
Marken, R. S. (1991). Degrees of freedom in behavior. *Psychological Science, 2*, 86–91.
Mayer-Kress, G., Newell, K. M., & Liu, Y.-T. (2009). Nonlinear dynamics of motor learning. *Nonlinear Dynamics, Psychology, and Life Sciences, 13*, 3–26.
Morrison, S., & Newell, K. M. (2015). Dimension and complexity in human movement and posture. *Nonlinear Dynamics, Psychology, & Life Sciences, 19*, 395–418.
Mykytyn, P. P., Jr. (1989). Group embedded figures test (GEFT): Individual differences, performance, and learning effects. *Educational and Psychological Measurement, 49*, 951–959.
Navarro, J., & Reuff-Lopes, R. (2015). Healthy variability in organizational behavior: Empirical evidence and new steps for future research. *Nonlinear Dynamics, Psychology, & Life Sciences, 19*, 529–552.
Navarro, J., Curioso, F., Gomes, G., Arrieta, C., & CortJs, M. (2013). Fluctuation in work motivation: Tasks do not matter! *Nonlinear Dynamics, Psychology, & Life Sciences, 17*, 3–22.
Peters, E. (1991). *Chaos and order in the capital markets*. New York: Wiley.
Peters, E. (1994). *Fractal market analysis: Applying chaos theory to investment and economics*. New York: Wiley.
Pincus, D. (2001). A framework and methodology for the study of nonlinear, self-organizing family dynamics. *Nonlinear Dynamics, Psychology, & Life Sciences, 5*, 139–174.

Pincus, D., & Metten, A. (2010). Nonlinear dynamics in biopsychosocial resilience. *Nonlinear Dynamics, Psychology, & Life Sciences, 14*, 353–380.

Rosenbaum, D. A., Slotta, J. D., Vaughn, J., & Plamondon, R. (1991). Optimal movement selection. *Psycholoical Science, 2*, 92–101.

Rosser, J. B., Jr. (1997). Speculations on nonlinear speculative bubbles. *Nonlinear Dynamics, Psychology, and Life Sciences, 1*, 275–300.

Rubinstein, J. S., Meyer, D. E., & Evans, J. E. (2001). Executive control of cognitive processes in task switching. *Journal of Experimental Psychology. Human Perception and Performance, 27*, 763–797.

Sheridan, T. B. (2002). *Human and automation: System design and research issues*. New York: Wiley.

Siad, I. A. (2001). Testing for nonlinear dynamics in the stock exchange of Thailand (SET). *ABAC Journal, 21*. Retrieved May 5, 2013, from www.journal.au.edu/abac_journal/2001/jan01/index.html

Sprott, J. C. (2003). *Chaos and time series analysis*. New York: Oxford University Press.

Sprott, J. C., & Rowlands, G. (2003). *The chaos data analyzer: The professional version*. New York: American Institute of Physics.

Stergiou, N., Harbourne, R. T., & Cavanaugh, J. T. (2006). Optimal movement variability: A new theoretical perspective for neurologic physical therapy. *Journal of Neurologic Physical Therapy, 30*, 120–129.

Stergiou, B., & Decker, L. M. (2011). Human movement variability, nonlinear dynamics, and pathology: Is there a connection? *Human Movement Science, 30*, 869–888.

Turvey, M. T. (1990). Coordination. *American Psychologist, 45*, 938–953.

Vargas, B., Cuesta-Frau, D., Ruiz-Esteban, R., Cinugeda, E., & Varela, M. (2015). What can biosignal entropy tell us about health and disease? Applications in some clinical fields. *Nonlinear Dynamics, Psychology, & Life Sciences, 19*, 419–436.

Weisstein, E. W. (1999). *CRC concise encyclopedia of mathematics*. Boca Raton: Chapman & Hall/CRC Press.

Chapter 6
The Performance-Variability Paradox: Risk Taking

Stephen J. Guastello

Abstract This study presented in this chapter extends the analyses and results from the previous chapter to the risk-taking aspect of the performance time series. Although the rescaled range statistic, H, is defined as having a range between 0 and 1, 24 % of the 172 time series were negative. Results confirmed that negative H was possible and not a result of psychometric error. Field dependence and H for the risk-taking time series were the best predictors of risk taking overall, of the variables studied. Persistence in risk taking, as evidenced by the autocorrelations was associated with spelling ability, anagrams test scores, and field dependence.

6.1 Introduction

The study presented in this chapter extends the previous one by examining the performance-variability paradox with regard to risk taking. The underlying issues are a bit different, however, with regard to risk taking. The classic studies on achievement motivation show that high achievers exhibit a moderate level of risk taking (McClelland 1961). They are not gamblers; they calculate the odds of success and make an informed decision, in much the same way as the participants in this running study have been asked to do.

Similarly, productivity among creative professionals appears to be highest for those with moderate risk taking tendencies (Guastello et al. 1998). Their cognitive styles tend to center on planning and re-planning the work, working through practical barriers to finishing the job, and the assembling idea elements that are already known to work in other contexts into a new product. The true innovators are actually taking a high level of risk in hopes of a big payoff. One difference between the manifestations of risk in the creative problem solving context compared to the context of securities trading is that the risk levels appear very different to the innovator compared to the rest of the world. Securities trading relies on the efficient

S.J. Guastello (✉)
Marquette University, Milwaukee, WI, USA
e-mail: Stephen.guastello@marquette.edu

S.J. Guastello (ed.), *Cognitive Workload and Fatigue in Financial Decision Making*, Evolutionary Economics and Social Complexity Science 13,
DOI 10.1007/978-4-431-55312-0_6

market assumption that all information that could possibly affect the price of the security is immediately reflected in the obvious price. (The assumption of an efficient market is often very questionable, but that is a matter that falls outside the scope of the present study.) The innovator relies on personal knowledge and experience to estimate risk associated with an endeavor, and that information is not widely shared for strategic reasons of maintaining competitive advantage.

Creative professionals, however, do engage in the same type of expectancy-prospect decisions when choosing projects to work on. They estimate the size of the "expected cheese" and, based on personal knowledge of what they can actually do, estimate the risks involved for each possible option. Then they choose the best option (Sternberg and Lubart 1995). It should be clear at this stage that some aspects of creative problem solving are actually optimizing in nature, and the results presented in the previous chapters indicate that the type of optimizing studied to this point works better without the creative input.

Given the known conflations between risk taking and optimizing, one can return to the more central question of whether there is an optimum level of variability in risk taking associated with performance in the financial decisions task. The other examples of optimum variability that were cited in the previous chapter were centered on performance of some sort. Risk taking is not a form of performance in that sense; it is an aspect of behavior that is concomitant with the central measure of performance. Nonetheless, the following hypotheses are testable now:

1. The Hurst exponents, H would tend toward anti-persistence and possibly negative values because of the bifurcation in the data that was first identified in the cusp models for risk taking in Chap. 3.
2. The negative values of H will be real and not a result of chance, using the same test with the standard error of measurement that was used previously.
3. The negative values of H will be associated with negative lag-1 autocorrelations are found previously.
4. The measures of total performance (optimizing) and total risk taking would be correlated with the variability of risk taking, signified by H, or the autocorrelations. This hypothesis is framed in the proverbial tongue-in-cheek fashion because of the incidental role of risk taking to total performance.

6.2 Method

The experimental procedure, participants, and measurements were described in Chap. 3. The participants for this segment were, once again, the 172 individuals who were assigned to experimental conditions in which they completed the series of 350 stimuli using the same two speed conditions: 15 s per item ($n = 102$), and 7.5 s per item ($n = 69$).

Measurements again included the timed tests of arithmetic, spelling, anagrams, and GEFT, and the untimed measures of anxiety, conscientiousness, PWE, and EI. For the analyses involving H, autocorrelations, and regression analyses, the full time series of 350 items was aggregated into 70 packets of 5 items, with a score ranging from 1 to 5 on each packet. The time series of 70 packets were analyzed with the Chaos Data Analyzer (Sprott and Rowlands 2003).

6.3 Results

6.3.1 Distribution of H

The H values for the 172 participants ranged from −0.09 to 0.29 (M = 0.032, SD = 0.058, SE = 0.004); 24 % of the H values were negative. Four examples of the risk taking time series appear in Fig. 6.1, three of which contained negative values of H and one was positive. They were selected for their distinctive appearances. All of the time series, however, showed a substantial hysteresis effect toward the end of series, similar to what occurred with the optimization criterion in the previous chapter.

The one-sample t-test showed that the mean of H was significantly different from zero (95 %CI: $0.024 < M < 0.040$). Once again the time series were strongly antipersistent, close to the lower limit of H.

The α reliability of the 70-item performance series was 0.96. The upper bound of the 95 % confidence interval around the lowest value of H was $H + [t_{(df=120)} * SEM_H] = -0.09 + 0.22 = -0.07$. Furthermore, 4.7 % of the sample produced values of H with upper bounds of their confidence intervals falling below 0.0. Thus the observed negative values of H are *not* the result of measurement error.

The lag-1 autocorrelations ranged from −0.20 to 0.53 (M = 0.141, SD = 0.161, SE = 0.012). The autocorrelations based on optimal lag ranged from −0.36 to 0.54 (M = 0.178, SD = 0.215, SE = 0.016). The lag length for the optimal autocorrelation ranged from 1 to 16 (M = 5.667, SD = 4.740, SE = 0.361).

The distributions of the four statistics are shown in Fig. 6.2. The distribution of H was normal-appearing again. Lag-1 autocorrelations were also normal-appearing, clustering close to 0.0, with a possible secondary mode at $r = 0.18$. This result suggested that there were some small but possibly important individual differences in serial memory operating.

The optimal autocorrelations were bimodally distributed with peaks at −0.22 and +0.25; the larger cluster was relatively persistent whereas the smaller group was antipersistent. The *lag* associated with optimal autocorrelations was 1 most often. The rest of the distribution resembled the inverse power law ($1/f^b$) except for the spike at lag 14. Furthermore, 51.5 % of the lags occurred at 4 or greater. A comparison of this distribution with the inverse power law showed that the degree of fit ($R^2 = 0.648$, $N = 15$ numerical categories) was not particularly good, however (see discussion).

The relationship between the negative H values and the direction of the autocorrelation were assessed next. The distribution of H was dichotomized between positive and negative values, as was the lag-1 autocorrelation; the breakdown of

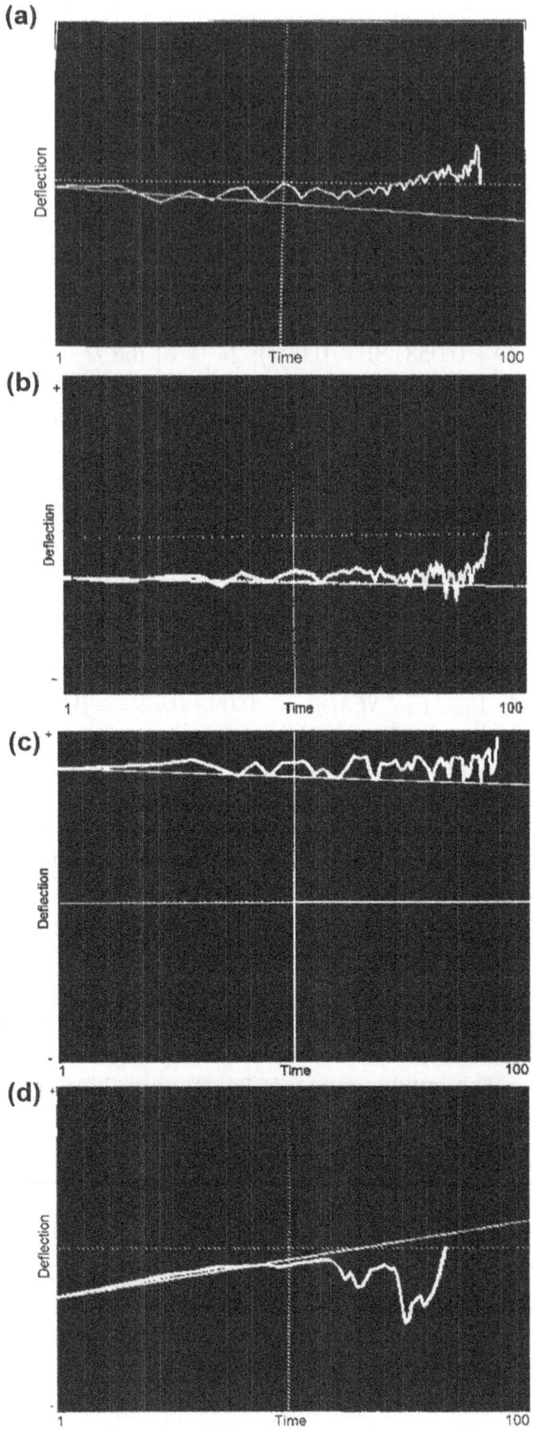

Fig. 6.1 Four examples of rescaled range times series for risk taking: (**a**) $H = -0.0887$, (**b**) $H = -0.0462$, (**c**) $H = -0.0389$, (**d**) $H = +0.2372$

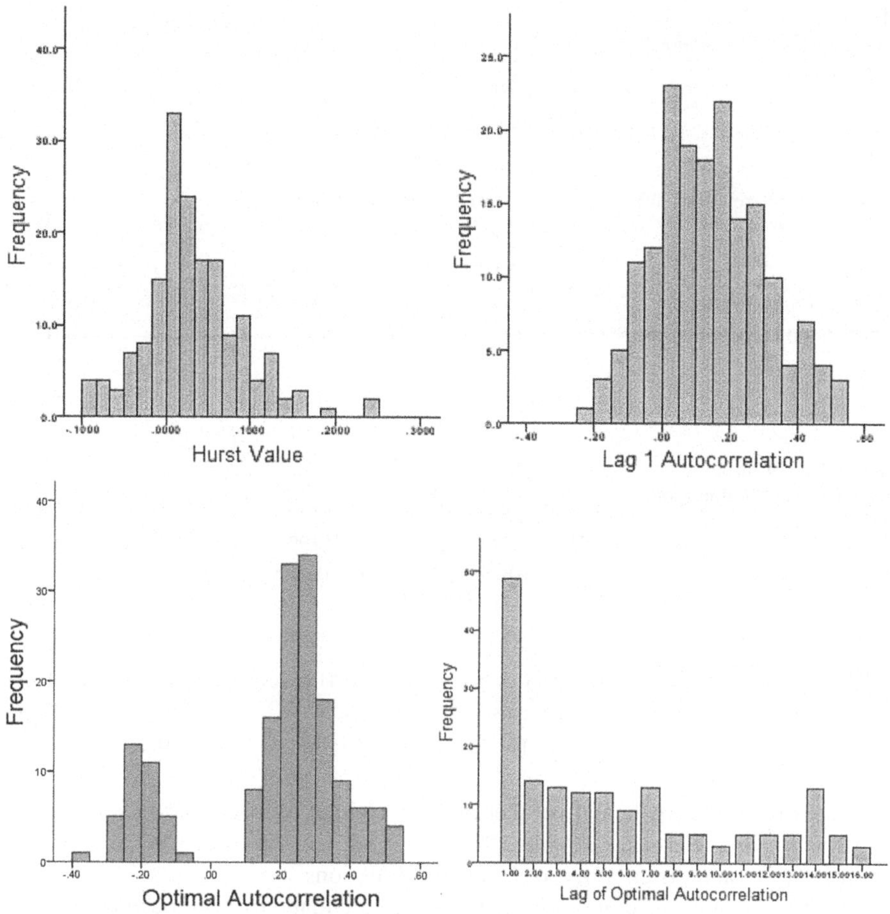

Fig. 6.2 Histograms of risk taking observations for H, the lag-1 autocorrelation, optimal autocorrelation, and optimal lag

frequencies appears in Table 6.1. A 2×2 χ^2 test showed that there was a clear association between negative or positive H and negative or positive lag-1 autocorrelation ($\chi^2 = 23.71$, $df = 1$, $p < 0.001$). The results again supported the conclusion that negative values of H result from time series that are negatively autocorrelated.

6.3.2 Regression Analyses

For these analyses, autocorrelations were transformed by their natural logs, such that $r'_{PP} = \ln(r_{PP} + 0.400)$. The correlations among the four statistics appear in Table 6.2. H was positively correlated with the lag-1 autocorrelation, which was

Table 6.1 Frequencies of H and Lag-1 autocorrelations for risk taking

	Lag-1 autocorrelations	
	Negative	Positive
H negative	14	28
H positive	19	111

Table 6.2 Correlations among structural variables for risk taking

	2	3	4
1. Hurst	0.417***	0.126	−0.245***
2. Lag-1 autocorrelation		0.300***	−0.535***
3. Optimal autocorrelation			−0.361***
4. Optimal lag			

*$p < 0.10$, **$p < 0.05$, ***$p < 0.01$

Table 6.3 Multiple regression predicting total risk taking

	β	*t*	R^2
Embedded figures	−0.186	−2.321**	0.031
Hurst (risk)	0.166	2.069**	0.058

*$p < 0.10$, **$p < 0.05$, ***$p < 0.01$

Table 6.4 Multiple regression predicting total performance

	β	*t*	R^2
Total risk taking	−0.412	−5.589****	0.176
Anagrams	−0.183	−2.216**	0.203

*$p < 0.10$, **$p < 0.05$, ***$p < 0.01$, ****$p < 0.001$

expected from the mathematical theory. The optimal autocorrelation was higher-positive for the shorter lag lengths. The longer lag lengths tended to be associated with antipersistent, oscillatory, or hysteresis functions.

A stepwise multiple regression analysis was calculated for total risk taking as the dependent measure. Total risk taking was the sum of the risky choices made over the entire time series. The independent variables were the ability tests, survey variables, TLX ratings, and *H*. Two variables accounted for the maximum amount of variance: field dependence and *H* ($R = 0.242$, adj. $R^2 = 0.046$, $F(2,149) = 4.562$, $p < 0.01$; Table 6.3). People who took more risks tended to be field dependent, which is consistent (or repetitive) with findings reported in previous chapters. Those who took more risks were also more persistent in doing so.

A stepwise multiple regression analysis was calculated for total performance (optimizing) as the dependent measure. The independent variables were total risk taking, the ability tests, survey variables, TLX ratings, and *H*. Two variables accounted for the maximum amount of variance, total risk taking and anagrams, both of which were negatively weighted ($R = 0.450$, adj. $R^2 = 0.192$, $F(2, 147) = 18.688$, $p < 0.001$; Table 6.4). People who optimized more often were those who took fewer risks and did not score so well on the anagrams test.

Stepwise multiple regression analyses were also conducted to determine if there were any predictors of the optimal autocorrelation for either risk taking or

Table 6.5 Multiple regression predicting optimal autocorrelation in optimizing performance

	β	*t*	R^2
Spelling	0.252	2.589**	0.073
Anagrams	0.215	2.221**	0.118
Embedded figures	−0.204	−2.218**	0.159

*$p < 0.10$, **$p < 0.05$

optimizing, which were both bimodally distributed. The independent variables were total risk taking, the ability tests, survey variables, and TLX ratings. There were no predictors, of those variables that were attempted, of optimal autocorrelation of risk taking. There were three predictors, however, of optimal autocorrelation for optimizing ($R = 0.399$, adj. $R^2 = 0.159$, $F(3, 93) = 5.856$, $p < 0.001$; Table 6.5). The principle predictors were spelling test scores (positive), anagrams (positive), and GEFT (negative).

6.4 Discussion

The first important finding was that negative values of *H* were again encountered, and it was possible to rule out measurement error as an explanation. The trend now seems to support the view that negative values of *H* arise from bifurcation effects within the data. The hysteresis that is associated with bifurcations that appear in catastrophe models is more severe than oscillations. A hysteresis effect has a stickiness that is produced by the stable states that are positioned to each side of the volatile range of the dependent measure. Oscillations, in contrast, are single attractors that do not involve a repellor or a bifurcation; the two phenomena might bear a close resemblance, however, and the properties of the system need to be studied deeply enough to draw the correct conclusion about the underlying dynamics (Guastello 1995; Guastello and Gregson 2011).

The second important finding involves the performance-variability paradox. In spite of the expressed skepticism, the variability of risk taking, as measured by *H*, was correlated with the total risk taking measure. The result provided further support for the hypothesis that there would be an optimal level of variability associated with high (desirable) levels of performance. Risk taking was not a targeted performance criterion, but a secondary one; risks are often necessary to achieve the performance objective.

An optimal risk position is relative to the situation. In the running experiment here, which was not the least bit life-threatening, the risky choice and the optimal choice were the same for 24 out of 175 different stimuli (13.7 %). The risky option was the one with the lowest odds of success, irrespective of the maximum expected outcome, as defined by the expectancy principle. Ten out of the 24 items appeared in the first block of 30 items (33.3 %), while the remaining 14 were distributed among the remaining 140 in the next four blocks of trials. The 24 possibilities were homogenously distributed within the 175 items in block 6. If the decision makers were optimizing effectively, the trends that were removed to produce the variance patterns in Fig. 6.1 would pitch downward, and the individual risk taking trend would zig-zag around the trend line; both events occurred often. The projected linear trends were based on a line drawn between the first (items 1–5) and the eighth (items 41–45) observations in the time series of 70 observations. Levels of risk taking beyond the expected levels would be an effect of natural biases of the participants before joining the experiment, workload or fatigue. The performance variability associated with fatigue is particularly salient in the volatile sequences of observations that occurred toward the end of the experimental sessions.

The multiple regression analysis using optimal autocorrelations as the criteria addressed the flip side of the performance-variability paradox by asking what explains the most rigid forms of stability. Consistency of performance is not synonymous with high levels of performance; consistency can occur at high, medium, and low levels. The latest research on the optimal variability hypothesis is showing that high levels of consistency are often associated with *rigidity* or compromised functionality (Bianciardi 2015; Corrêa et al. 2015; Guastello 2015; Harrison and Stergiou 2015; Kiefer and Myer 2015; Morrison and Newell 2015; Navarro and Rueff-Lopes 2015; Vargas et al. 2015; Schuldberg 2015). In the case of optimizing, the most consistent participants expressed the opposite abilities or traits that were associated with top-level performance.

Finally, for this chapter, the distribution of lag lengths that were associated with the optimal autoregression coefficients for the individual time series appeared to be distributed as inverse power laws, but the degree of fit was relatively low. In actuality, subjective or objective norms for tests of distributional fit have never been firmly established. At present, an $R^2 > 0.85$ would be convincing barring a better alternative theory for the statistical distribution (Guastello 2005). Exponential, log-normal, power law, and Poisson distributions can look very similar. In ambiguous cases an assumption of one distribution or another afford advantages for statistical analysis, but could obviate other opportunities or interpretations of data. A power law distribution, should it be confirmed, would support the view that a self-organizing process was involved in the individual time series. Another question would be to identify *what* cognitive processes self-organized. Under the present circumstances, however, it does not appear that such an investigation would afford any new knowledge about cognitive workload, fatigue, and decision biases that have not been identified already.

References

Bianciardi, G. (2015). Differential diagnosis: Shape and function, fractal tools in the pathology lab. *Nonlinear Dynamics, Psychology, and Life Sciences, 19*, 437–464.

Corrêa, U. C., Benda, R. N., de Oliveira, D., Ugrinowitsch, H., Freudenheim, A. M., & Tani, G. (2015). Different faces of variability in the adaptive process of motor skill learning. *Nonlinear Dynamics, Psychology, and Life Sciences, 19*, 465–488.

Guastello, S. J. (2005). Statistical distributions and self-organizing phenomena: What conclusions should be drawn? *Nonlinear Dynamics, Psychology, and Life Sciences, 9*, 463–478.

Guastello, S. J. (2015). The complexity of the psychological self and the principle of optimum variability. *Nonlinear Dynamics, Psychology, and Life Sciences, 19*, 511–528.

Guastello, S. J., & Gregson, R. A. M. (Eds.). (2011). *Nonlinear dynamical systems analysis for the behavioral sciences using real data*. Boca Raton: C R C Press/Taylor & Francis.

Guastello, S. J. (1995). *Chaas, catastrophe, and human affairs*. Mahwah: Lawrence Erlbaum Associates.

Guastello, S. J., Shissler, J., Driscoll, J., & Hyde, T. (1998). Are some cognitive styles more creatively productive than others? *Journal of Creative Behavior, 32*, 77–91.

Harrison, S. J., & Stergiou, N. (2015). Complex adaptive behavior in dexterous action. *Nonlinear Dynamics, Psychology, and Life Sciences, 19*, 345–394.

Kiefer, A. W., & Myer, G. D. (2015). Training the anti-fragile athlete: A preliminary analysis of neuromuscular training effects on muscle activation dynamics. *Nonlinear Dynamics, Psychology, and Life Sciences, 19*, 489–511.

McClelland, D. C. (1961). *The achieving society*. Princeton: Van Nostrand.

Morrison, S., & Newell, K. M. (2015). Dimension and complexity in human movement and posture. *Nonlinear Dynamics, Psychology, and Life Sciences, 19*.

Navarro, J., & Rueff-Lopes, R. (2015). Healthy variability in organizational behavior: Empirical evidence and new steps for future research. *Nonlinear Dynamics, Psychology, and Life Sciences, 19*, 529–552.

Schuldberg, D. (2015). What is optimum variability? *Nonlinear Dynamics, Psychology, and Life Sciences, 19*, 553–568.

Sprott, J. C., & Rowlands, G. (2003). *The chaos data analyzer: The professional version*. New York: American Institute of Physics.

Sternberg, R. J., & Lubart, T. I. (1995). *Defying the crowd: Cultivating creativity in a culture of conformity*. New York: Free Press.

Vargas, B., Cuesta-Frau, D., Ruiz-Esteban, R., Cirugeda, E., & Varela, M. (2015). What can biosignal entropy tell us about health and disease? Applications in some clinical fields. *Nonlinear Dynamics, Psychology, and Life Sciences, 19*, 419–436.

Chapter 7
Determining Optimization-Risk Profiles for Individual Decision Makers

Stephen J. Guastello and Anthony F. Peressini

Abstract Investment funds typically vary with regard to the emphasis that the managers place on acceptable risk and expected returns on investment. This chapter highlight a nonlinear analytic strategy, orbital decomposition (ORBDE) for identifying and extracting patterns of categorical events from time series data. The contributing constructs from symbolic dynamics, chaos, and entropy are described in conjunction with the central ORBDE algorithm. A study in task switching, which can alleviate or induce cognitive fatigue, is used an illustrative example of the basic mode of analysis. The aggregate more of ORBDE allows category codes from multiple variables to be assigned to each event in a time series. An illustrative example of the aggregate mode is presented for risk profile analysis in financial decisions. The results open up many possibilities for studying sequences of decisions made by fund managers and individual investors to determine profiles of risk acceptance, expected returns, and other features of portfolio management.

7.1 Introduction

Financial experts of different types often speak of a risk profile that describes how they (or their clients) distribute their preferences for assets that contain varying amount of risk relative to expected returns. For instance a mutual fund for corporate stocks would contain a mix of stocks trading on fundamentals and those that have speculative potential; their market values would reflect a range of price-equity ratios. Bond funds would contain a mix of holdings that range from those that are very secure and pay relatively low dividends to those that are very sketchy but offering higher dividends. Portfolios composed by individuals for their own use (i.e., they are not working for a fund or trying to attract other investors), have similar types of distributions and balance points. The objective of this chapter is to describe a method for determining such a profile for an individual decision maker.

S.J. Guastello (✉) • A.F. Peressini
Marquette University, Milwaukee, WI, USA
e-mail: Stephen.guastello@marquette.edu

S.J. Guastello (ed.), *Cognitive Workload and Fatigue in Financial Decision Making*, Evolutionary Economics and Social Complexity Science 13,
DOI 10.1007/978-4-431-55312-0_7

The restricting condition for purposes of this demonstration is that the individual was left to his or her own devices and was not constrained by a portfolio management policy. One could extrapolate the method to collective judgments of teams as they make a series of decisions that are relevant to the needs of a defined fund.

Analyses that are similar to the example presented here are sometimes known as *policy capturing regression*. "Regression" in this context refers to multiple linear regression most often. In the prototype analyses for policy capturing, the data base would contain many data frames consisting of input variables and decision outcomes. The statistical analysis produces a set of regression weights that were implicit in the decisions that were already made, and they are meant to be used again to make further decisions that are consistent with the existing batch. An example policy question might be, "How much should we pay each employee based on the actual content of their jobs and years of experience?" The data base would contain job analysis numbers, perhaps five of them, that represent properties of jobs. The dependent measure would be current pay, howsoever it was determined in the past. The multiple regression analysis would produce a linear equation that translates job evaluation factors and experience into current pay. That regression model can be used to compare predicted with actual outcomes to detect errors in the current compensation structure and to establish fair pay rates for new jobs and employees.

The greatest advantage of the regression method is also its greatest limitation. It isolates one rule that best accounts for all decisions that are fed into the statistical analysis. By definition, it does not portray a spectrum of decisions as would be associated with profiles.

The problem that is posed by risk-optimization profiles is structurally similar to problems addressed by policy capturing regression in the sense that decisions are made on available data (the experimental stimuli), there is a pattern that accounts for the individual's decisions, and the pattern can be extracted through statistical analysis. The profiling situation is different from the examples of job evaluation and compensation in three ways, however. First, there is a profile of two outcomes, optimization and risk taking, instead of a single outcome on a continuous scale. Second, we are not analyzing the properties of all decisions made by all decision makers, but looking for a pattern within each decision maker's data individually; the central features of the individual analyses can be compared further across individuals if desired. Third, the decisions are made in a steady stream, and thus conditions of varying workload and fatigue are involved.

What follows is actually a demonstration of a possible technique with one case and a two-variable outcome. The analysis, known as orbital decomposition (ORBDE) is based on symbolic dynamics and makes use of entropy constructs, which are closely tied to nonlinear dynamical systems. It has been used for many interesting applications outside of financial decision making. Some background on entropy is provided next, followed by the properties of ORBDE itself and the example for profiling optimization and risk taking preferences.

7.2 Entropy

The entropy construct underwent some important developments since it was introduced in the late nineteenth century. Initially, it meant "heat loss." This definition led to the principle that systems will eventually dissipate heat and expire from "heat death." A century later, this generalization turned out to be incorrect, when it was discovered that systems respond to high entropy conditions by self-organizing (Haken 1984; Prigogine and Stengers 1984).

The second perspective originated in the early twentieth century with statistical physics. It was not possible to target individual molecules for measurement, but it was possible to define metrics of the average motion of the molecules. The third perspective was that of Shannon entropy: A system can take on any of a number of discrete states over time. It takes *information* to predict those states, and any variability for which information is not available to predict is considered entropy. Entropy and information add up to H_{MAX}, maximum information, which occurs when all the states of a system have equal probabilities of occurrence:

$$H_s = \sum\nolimits_{\text{i}} [p_i \log_2(1/p_i)],$$

where i is a system state and p is the probability of that state (Shannon 1948).

The NDS perspective on entropy, however, is that entropy is generated *by* a system as it changes behavior over time (Nicolis and Prigogine 1989; Prigogine and Stengers 1984) and thus it has become commonplace to treat Shannon information and Shannon entropy as interchangeable quantities. Other measures of entropy have been developed for different types of NDS problems. *Topological entropy* is the construct of choice here because it is the end result of the pattern detection algorithm in ORBDE (Lathrop and Kostelich 1989). There is a limiting relationship between topological entropy and the largest Lyapunov exponent. Lastly, Kolmogorov-Sinai entropy was also developed as a form of topological entropy, but it requires ordered sets of categories along two or more pre-defined axes. However, it becomes useful with the aggregated functions with ORBDE.

7.3 Orbital Decomposition

7.3.1 Symbolic Dynamics

Symbolic dynamics is a branch of mathematics that manipulates patterns of events. The events can originate in numerical sources, but the qualitative patterns are the central concern here. For instance, we can have two functions

$$f_1(X), X : \{A, B, C, D, \ldots\},$$
$$f_2(X), X : \{A, B, C, D, \ldots\},$$

and then a function *g* that manipulates the two functions of X:

$$g(X), f = \{f_1(X), f_2(X)\}.$$

Principles of symbolic dynamics are widely applied in computer science and have found a home in genetics research (e.g. Jiménez-Montaño et al. 2004). For instance if we have a series of genetic codes

A B C A B C D E F G A B C,

we look for repeating sequences and the pattern that governs when they appear. In broad contexts, the choice of algorithm depends on what one is looking for, how it is expected to appear in the raw data source, and how one wants to estimate the optimal length of the "word," object, or *string* (underlined sequences ABC above).

The ORBDE technique, which was first developed by Guastello et al. (1998), empirically determines the content of patterns and makes direct links to other useful measurements such as entropy, the Lyapunov exponent, and the fractal dimension. Applications of ORBDE have included creative problem solving discussions (Guastello 2000; Guastello et al. 1998), family and group therapy dynamics, (Pincus 2001, 2014; Pincus and Guastello 2005; Pincus et al. 2008; 2011), political violence, (Spohn 2008), intimate partner violence (Katerndahl et al. 2010, 2015) the contents of medical interviews (Katerndahl and Parchman 2010), self-injuring behavior (Pincus et al. 2014), neuromotor activation patterns (Nathan et al. 2012), and task-switching, multi-tasking, and work performance (Guastello et al. 2012; 2013).

7.3.2 ORBDE Standard Mode

ORBDE is a symbolic dynamics analysis that identifies recurring patterns of events in nominally coded data. The concept for the analysis (Guastello et al. 1998) originated with the assumption that a chaotic sequence of observations originates with coupled oscillators (orbits) and thus the goal is to decouple the contributing oscillators (Lathrop and Kostelich 1989). There are actually three principle pathways to chaos from non-chaotic systems: forcing a point through a field containing multiple attractors, inducing bifurcations of particular types, and coupling oscillators. ORBDE exploits the third possibility. If we take a pendulum, pin-joint it to two other pendulums (Fig. 7.1) and then activate Pendulum 1, the other two pendulums will oscillate chaotically. More broadly, three coupled oscillators are sufficient to produce chaos (Newhouse et al. 1978), although not all possible combinations of oscillators and parameters will do so (Puu 1993), and some oscillators can become unstable in the presence of others (Puu 2000). Nonetheless that is exactly the

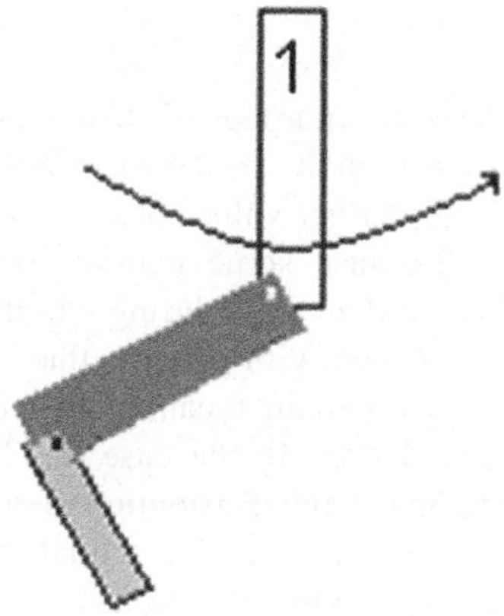

Fig. 7.1 A possible scenario for three coupled oscillators

morass of possibilities that can be analyzed with symbolic dynamics (Guastello et al. 1998; Lathrop and Kostelich 1989; Robinson 1999).

ORBDE does not *assume* chaos or require that the data be chaotic, but it can accommodate chaotic levels of complexity. The analysis finds the optimal length of patterns (string length, or C), and the recurring patterns at that string length. The search for optimal string length is based on whether any patterns proximally recur; i.e., a particular pattern appears immediately after itself:

$$H_t = \lim_{C\to\infty}(1/C)\log_2(\mathbf{trM})$$

where **trM** is the number of patterns that proximally recur. It is actually the trace of a square matrix **M** of all patterns followed by all other patterns. For each matrix entry we enter 1 if a pattern follows another and 0 otherwise. The trace is the sum of diagonal elements and is equal to the number of distinct patterns that follow themselves immediately. The limit is taken by calculating Ht for values of C as C increases. Once **trM** goes to 0, the analysis backs up to the last step where $\mathbf{trM} > 0$, and the corresponding value of C is taken as the optimal string length for the time series.

Once the length has been determined, the patterns that appear at least twice – proximally or distally – are identified. The final statistics include string length, topological entropy (Ht), the Lyapunov dimension, D_L; Shannon entropy, Hs, and a maximum likelihood chi-square test for goodness of fit:

$$\chi^2 = 2\sum[F_{\mathrm{Ob}}\ln(F_{\mathrm{Ob}}/F_{\mathrm{Ex}})].$$

The χ^2 test compares the observed frequency of a pattern against the number of examples of that pattern that would be expected F_{Ex} based on the combinatorial odds for each of the contributing event codes. For instance, if an observed pattern involved events I, J, and K:

$$F_{\text{Ex}} = p_I p_J p_K N^*.$$

N^* is the number of strings that were parsed from the data series. The asterisk is used to indicate that the number of strings becomes gradually smaller as progressively larger values of C (string length) are tested.

Because some patterns occur only rarely and some possibilities might not materialize at all during a finite time series, the observed and expected frequencies associated with patterns that appear exactly once are combined into one category (equivalent in meaning to "none of the above strings") for purposes of the χ^2 calculation. In the case of $C = 1$, where there are no combinations, the χ^2 test compares the distribution of codes or objects to the hypothesis of equal probability.

Similarly, when the final string length has been determined, the researcher can go back to the preliminary statistics associated with that particular string length and interpret their meaning. Only strings that appear at least twice are interpreted. Some example sets of final statistics from an ORBDE analysis of data collected from four participants in a task-switching study (Guastello et al. 2012) appear in Table 7.1. Participants #19 and 25 adopted strategies of two-task sequences, Participant #26 used a three-task strategy, and Participant #24 used a seven-task strategy. The actual task sequences deployed by Participants 19 and 24 appear in Table 7.2. The letter codes refer to the names of the seven tasks. The column "repeat?" indicates whether the string was one that immediately repeated itself.

7.3.3 *Well-Behaved and Ill-Behaved Data*

In the prototype, or *well-behaved* data series, *Ht* decreases gradually to 0 or undefined as C increases. The final statistics for Participants 19, 25, and 26 would be examples of well-behaved data in which ORBDE is untangling coupled oscillators. Four types of *ill-behaved* data have also been identified (Guastello et al. 2011):

1. The case where *Ht* decreases gradually up to a point, then increases suddenly and decreases again. This type of event is a sign of a hierarchical periodic oscillator. Participant 24 in Table 7.2 displayed one of many plausible examples, in which the 7-unit patterns were hierarchical over the 2-unit patterns. For instance, a person might display a few different behavioral patterns within a day, but each *day* is a virtual repetition of the previous day.
2. The final results start to look well-behaved as C increases, but **trM** lingers on 1 for several values of C before the algorithm terminates. This type of result indicates a long series of one event code that is potentially dominating the rest of the data series. In this condition the χ^2 test can be informative for deciding whether to conclude that the final string length for purposes of interpreting the other strings should be shorter than the final value of C. Here one would look for the highest χ^2 value in the ambiguous range of C.

Table 7.1 Sample ORBDE final statistics

C	trM	*Ht*	D_L	χ^2	*df*	*N**	*Hs*
S19							
1	7	2.807	16.566	0.130	6	48	1.945
2	2	0.500	1.649	32.333	11	47	3.275
S24							
1	7	2.807	16.566	0.000	6	49	1.946
2	7	1.404	4.070	96.739	15	48	2.766
7	2	0.143	1.154	76.811	2	43	3.697
S25							
1	7	2.807	16.566	0.000	6	49	1.946
2	6	1.292	3.642	78.875	7	48	2.750
S26							
1	7	2.807	16.566	0.000	6	49	1.946
2	7	1.404	4.070	106.358	13	48	2.629
3	5	0.774	2.168	139.019	7	47	3.120

Reprinted from Guastello et al. (2012, p. 484) with permission of the Society for Chaos Theory in Psychology & Life Sciences

Table 7.2 Task patterns deployed by two participants from Table 7.1

Code		Repeat?	Freq	Ex Freq
S19	TT	Yes	4	1.000
	SS	–	3	1.000
	RR	–	3	1.000
	AA	–	3	0.734
	CR	Yes	3	1.000
	CC	–	2	1.000
	PP	–	2	1.000
	PM	–	2	1.000
	MA	–	2	0.857
	AC	–	2	0.857
	PT	–	2	1.000
(Followed by 19 doublets that appeared only once)				
S24	MACRSPT	Yes	2	0.000
	ACRSPTM	Yes	2	0.000
(Followed by 39 7-character strings that appeared only once)				

Reprinted from Guastello et al. (2012, p. 485) with permission of the Society for Chaos Theory in Psychology & Life Sciences

3. There is a single oscillator such as ABCDE_ABCDE_ABCDE... Here one would see in the final statistics no immediate repetitions until $C = 5$, after which the further values of C would be multiples of 5.
4. Random data can be detected when C does not increase past 1 and the χ^2 test is not significant.

7.4 ORBDE Aggregated Mode for Profiling

The ORBDE examples considered so far involved the use of one categorical variable for which the categories were mutually exclusive. This standard mode of ORBDE can accommodate 52 event codes corresponding to the 26 letters of the alphabet, upper and lower case. ORBDE, v2.4 (Peressini and Guastello 2014) contains a feature that allows the researcher to assign multiple codes from one set of categories to an event, or to apply category codes from multiple variables to each event. When working in the standard mode, ORBDE reads each single *keystroke* as an event. When working in the aggregation modes, however, ORBDE reads a *line* of data as an event. In the first part of the aggregation process ORBDE tallies the lines of code patterns and renames each one as a single letter. The standard ORBDE routine is then applied to the new set of single letter codes.

The output gives a table that shows the conversion of the elementary lines of code to single aggregate codes, the preliminary statistics based on the aggregate single-character codes in the format of Table 7.2, and the final statistics based on the aggregate codes in the format of Table 7.1. The new element that is reported here is Kolmogorov-Sinai entropy, which is another measure of topological entropy. Its value is essentially Shannon entropy for one- or two-variable problems (Heath 2000; Sprott 2003). For three or more variables, Kolmogorov-Sinai entropy requires variables that are ordered categories, and its value diverges from Shannon entropy. Like Shannon entropy, however, it is not responsive to temporal sequencing of events.

The example of decision profiling that follows uses the aggregation routine to determine patterns in data sets where there are multiple categorical variables and a code from each variable that can be applied to an event. An option in ORBDE converts any aggregate codes that appear only once to a common code (lower-case-z). This option can bring clarity to an ambiguous solution. The profiling example presented in this chapter used multiple (2) categorical values, each with six categories, with the common code command. The data were the responses of one participant whose data were already prepared for use in the analyses appearing in Chaps. 5 and 6.

Data consisted of one of the time series from Chaps. 5 and 6. There were 70 observations, and each observation was a packet of five decisions. Risk and optimization were initially valued on a 0–5 scale. For ORBDE analysis the values 0–5 were changed to A–E respectively. The list of risk-optimization pairs that occurred appear in Table 7.3 (risk preceding optimization). The most common combination that represents this decision maker's dominant strategy was BD (or 1, 4), which was replaced by the aggregate code L. L appeared 12 times. The next two most frequent combinations were AE and BC, which appeared six times each. There were four aggregate codes that appeared only once; those were represented by the common code z.

The solution for this analysis was $C = 2$ using both the *Ht* and χ^2 criteria. (Table 7.4). The list of aggregated code sequences for $C = 2$ is shown in Table 7.5.

Table 7.3 Frequency distributions of code combinations for the risk profile problem using the common code subcommand

	Aggregated		
Original Code Combination (Risk, Optimizing)	Code	Number	Frequency
DE	A	5	0.071
AE	B	6	0.086
DF	C	3	0.043
CE	D	5	0.071
BF	E	3	0.043
CF	F	3	0.043
EF	G	2	0.029
CC	H	5	0.071
CA	z	1	0.014
DB	z	1	0.014
DD	z	1	0.014
BC	I	6	0.086
BB	J	2	0.029
CB	K	3	0.043
BD	L	12	0.171
AC	M	2	0.029
CD	N	2	0.029
DC	z	1	0.014
BE	O	5	0.071
AD	P	2	0.029

Reprinted from Peressini and Guastello (2014) with permission of the authors. Annotations added

The aggregate code L was followed by another L five times. This self-repetition defined the solution to the pattern length. There were other patterns that appeared two or three times, notable LI and IL. Both I and L involved the same risk level (low), but optimization waffled somewhat. There were also bursts of risky choices (aggregate zz), which were probably located toward the high-fatigue end of the time series. There were many sequences that appeared only once, so only the first is listed in this excerpt from the output.

Table 7.4 Revised final statistics for the risk profile problem using the common code subcommand

C	trM	Ht	D_L	χ^2	df	N*	Hs
1	8	3.000	20.086	20.198	16	70	2.689
2	1	0.000	1.000	36.768	9	69	3.901

Reprinted from Peressini and Guastello (2014) with permission of the authors

Table 7.5 Patterns of aggregates for the risk profile problem using the common code subcommand

Code (C = 2)	Repeat?	Freq	Ex Freq	Pr-Obs
LL	y	5	2.028	0.072
LI	–	3	1.014	0.043
IL	–	3	1.014	0.043
zz	–	2	0.225	0.029
zI	–	2	0.338	0.029
KL	–	2	0.507	0.029
HE	–	2	0.211	0.029
HB	–	2	0.422	0.029
OO	–	2	0.352	0.029
CA	–	1	62.889	0.014

7.5 Further Uses of Pattern Profiles

The ORBDE algorithm extract temporal patterns of categorical variables and produces entropy metrics to accompany the final set of patterns. A χ^2 statistic determines if the patterns could have occurred by chance. The central algorithm starts with the assumption that the original data stream resulted from coupled oscillators and proceeds to untangle them. ORBDE also performs well with "ill-behaved" data that are composed from simple oscillators or hierarchically organized oscillators; symptoms of these dynamical patterns are evident in the patterns of final statistics that are associated with the solutions at different pattern lengths. ORBDE can also disentangle patterns from time series that contain multiple codes per observation through the use of aggregate functions.

Illustrative applications included here involved task switching, which only required one categorical variable for analysis, and risk-optimization profiling, which was a two-variable problem. The task switching example was particularly relevant to cognitive workload and fatigue, although the application involved seven perceptual-motor tasks rather than the mental calculations that usually go with risk-optimization decisions. In theory, task switching can alleviate fatigue when the operator has been working on one task for too long, but switching can also induce fatigue because of the need to change mental schemata or to keep two or more schemata in mind at the same time. The interim conclusion from the human factors literature is now that switching is beneficial for performance so long as it occurs at the operator's discretion, but switching that is induced by automation or uncontrollable interruptions can be detrimental. It is now possible to open up a new range of questions concerning optimal task switching strategies for people working in the financial industries.

Future research on profiles could be studied in a more complex fashion by taking into account other properties of assets such as whether they are stocks, bonds, or commodities; originating from different industry groups; target profiles for a fund; and diversity of industry classifications. If one were to compare people, one might find clusters of profiles. From there one could conduct further analyses using many of the same individual difference variables that were used in previous chapters to distinguish the individual's profiles. In the present situation, we were only concerned with two variables in a profile and already did some extensive analyses to determine how those behavioral outcomes respond to workload and fatigue manipulations and individual differences, so there did not appear to be much additional utility in repeating the illustrative analysis 170 times.

If one were to analyze decisions made by a fund, perhaps as results of team decisions, it would be possible to profile the decisions that were actually made by the fund and compare them to the stated objectives. Analyses of funds would have to take into account that good deals on markets are not always well-timed with the cash position for taking advantage of them. It is a dubious day in the life of a fund manager to have a sudden influx of cash from new investments and not have a good place to park it. In any case, some further possibilities for putting profiling techniques to good use are considered in the next chapter.

References

Guastello, S. J. (2000). Symbolic dynamic patterns of written exchange: Hierarchical structures in an electronic problem solving group. *Nonlinear Dynamics, Psychology, and Life Sciences, 4*, 169–188.

Guastello, S. J., Hyde, T., & Odak, M. (1998). Symbolic dynamic patterns of verbal exchange in a creative problem solving group. *Nonlinear Dynamics, Psychology, and Life Sciences, 2*, 35–58.

Guastello, S. J., Peressini, A. F., & Bond, R. W., Jr. (2011). Orbital decomposition for ill-behaved event sequences: Transients and superordinate structures. *Nonlinear Dynamics, Psychology, and Life Sciences, 15*, 465–476.

Guastello, S. J., Gorin, H., Huschen, S., Peters, N. E., Fabisch, M., & Poston, K. (2012). New paradigm for task switching strategies while performing multiple tasks: Entropy and symbolic dynamics analysis of voluntary patterns. *Nonlinear Dynamics, Psychology, and Life Sciences, 16*, 471–497.

Guastello, S. J., Gorin, H., Huschen, S., Peters, N. E., Fabisch, M., Poston, K., & Weinberger, K. (2013). The minimum entropy principle and task performance. *Nonlinear Dynamics, Psychology, and Life Sciences, 17*, 405–424.

Haken, H. (1984). *The science of structure: Synergetics*. New York: Van Nostrand Reinhold.

Heath, R. A. (2000). *Nonlinear dynamics: Techniques and applications in psychology*. Mahwah: Erlbaum.

Jiménez-Montaño, M. A., Feistel, R., & Diez-Martínez, O. (2004). Information hidden in signals and macromolecules I. Symbolic time-series analysis. *Nonlinear Dynamics, Psychology, and Life Sciences, 8*, 445–478.

Katerndahl, D. A., & Parchman, M. L. (2010). Dynamical differences in patient encounters involving uncontrolled diabetes. *Journal of Evaluation in Clinical Practice, 16*, 211–219.

Katerndahl, D., Ferrer, R., Burge, S., Becho, J., & Wood, R. (2010). Recurrent patterns of daily intimate partner violence and environment. *Nonlinear Dynamics, Psychology, and Life Sciences, 14*, 511–524.

Katerndahl, D., Burge, S., Ferrer, R., Becho, J., & Wood, R. (2015). Recurrent multi-day patterns of intimate partner violence and alcohol intake in violent relationships. *Nonlinear Dynamics, Psychology, and Life Sciences, 19*, 41–63.

Lathrop, D. P., & Kostelich, E. J. (1989). Characterization of an experimental strange attractor by periodic orbits. *Physics Review, 40*, 4028–4031.

Nathan, D. E., Guastello, S. J., Prost, R. W., & Jeutter, D. C. (2012). Understanding neuromotor strategy during functional upper extremity tasks using symbolic dynamics. *Nonlinear Dynamics, Psychology, and Life Sciences, 16*, 37–59.

Newhouse, R., Ruelle, D., & Takens, F. (1978). Occurrence of strange attractors: An axiom near quasi-periodic flows on T^m, $m \geq 3$. *Communications in Mathematical Physics, 64*, 35–41.

Nicolis, G., & Prigogine, I. (1989). *Exploring complexity*. New York: Freeman.

Peressini, A. F., & Guastello, S. J. (2014). *Orbital decomposition: A short user's guide to ORBDE v2.4*. [Software]. Retrieved May 1, 2014, from http://www.societyforchaostheory.org/resources/. Menu 4.

Pincus, D. (2001). A framework and methodology for the study of nonlinear, self-organizing family dynamics. *Nonlinear Dynamics, Psychology, and Life Sciences, 5*, 139–174.

Pincus, D. (2014). One bad apple: Experimental effects of psychological conflict on social resilience. *Interface Focus, 4*, 20014003.

Pincus, D., & Guastello, S. J. (2005). Nonlinear dynamics and interpersonal correlates of verbal turn-taking patterns in group therapy. *Small Group Research, 36*, 635–677.

Pincus, D., Fox, K. M., Perez, K. A., Turner, J. S., & McGee, A. R. (2008). Nonlinear dynamics of individual and interpersonal conflict in an experimental group. *Small Group Research, 39*, 150–178.

Pincus, D., Ortega, D. L., & Metten, A. (2011). Orbital decomposition for multiple time series comparisons. In S. J. Guastello & R. A. M. Gregson (Eds.), *Nonlinear dynamical systems analysis for the behavioral sciences using real data* (pp. 517–538). Boca Raton: CRC Press.

Pincus, D., Eberle, K., Walder, C. S., Kemp, A. S., Lanjavi, M., & Sandman, C. A. (2014). The role of self-injury in behavioral flexibility and resilience. *Nonlinear Dynamics, Psychology, and Life Sciences, 18*, 277–296.

Prigogine, I., & Stengers, I. (1984). *Order out of chaos: Man's new dialog with nature*. New York: Bantam.

Puu, T. (1993). *Nonlinear economic dynamics* (3rd ed.). New York: Springer.

Puu, T. (2000). *Attractors, bifurcation and chaos: Nonlinear phenomena in economics*. New York: Springer.

Robinson, C. (1999). *Dynamical systems: Stability, symbolic dynamics, and chaos* (2nd ed.). Boca Raton: CRC Press.

Shannon, C. E. (1948). A mathematical theory of communication. *Bell System Technical Journal, 27*, 379–423.

Spohn, M. (2008). Violent societies: An application of orbital decomposition to the problem of human violence. *Nonlinear Dynamics, Psychology, and Life Sciences, 12*, 87–115.

Sprott, J. C. (2003). *Chaos and time series analysis*. Oxford: New York.

Chapter 8
Lessons Learned and Future Directions

Stephen J. Guastello

Abstract This chapter summarizes what has been learned about the dynamics of cognitive workload and fatigue and the extensions of the two cusp models to financial decision making in which an element of risk is involved. Other interesting findings concerning individual differences in response to cognitive workload and fatigue and the performance-variability paradox followed from the study of the two models. The last section of the chapter considers new directions for research that encompass greater levels of complexity that are found in the broader scope of financial decision making.

8.1 Cusp Models

Table 8.1 summarizes the cognitive workload and fatigue studies that have been conducted thus far with the two cusp models, including the study presented in Chap. 3. In the latter case, the results of the main study that spanned all blocks of the experimental stimuli contributed two pairs of R^2 coefficients (one for optimization and one for risk taking), and the results for the five blocks analyzed separately were averaged to produce two more pairs of results. Although a detailed discussion of the tasks is tempting, most tasks that have been studied are only tangentially related to financial decision making, so the interested reader is referred to the original sources in the footnotes to the table. They do cover a range of cognitive processes and demands on memory functions that are relevant to other types of work, however. Nonetheless, the average R^2 for the cusp models was .44 and the average R^2 for the best linear comparison models was .28. Thus about one-third of the variance accounted for by the cusp model is associated with the nonlinear dynamical structure.

Throughout the series of studies leading up to this one, it was apparent that the effects of workload on performance changes are sometime stronger than the effects

S.J. Guastello (✉)
Marquette University, Milwaukee, WI, USA
e-mail: Stephen.guastello@marquette.edu

S.J. Guastello (ed.), *Cognitive Workload and Fatigue in Financial Decision Making*, Evolutionary Economics and Social Complexity Science 13,
DOI 10.1007/978-4-431-55312-0_8

Table 8.1 Summary of results for cusp models for cognitive workload and fatigue

Model	Type of task	R^2 Cusp	R^2 Linear[a]	Bifurcation	Asymmetry
Workload	Episodic memory[b]	0.44	0.32	*Unknown*	Peak load
Fatigue	Episodic memory	0.53	0.50	Intervening work	Arithmetic
					Peak load
Workload	Pictorial memory[c]	0.53	0.13	Anxiety	Incentive condition
Fatigue	Episodic memory	0.30	0.16	*Unknown*	*Unknown*
	Episodic peak	0.39	0.07	*Unknown*	*Unknown*
	Pictorial memory	0.52	0.59	Intervening work	Episodic peak
Workload	Multitask @ Time 1[d]	0.49	0.35	*Unknown*	Task difficulty
	Multitask @ Time 2	0.75	0.18	Self-determined task order	*Unknown*
Fatigue	Accuracy	0.47	0.56	Fully alternating order	Spelling
				Self-determined task order	
	Memory	0.53	0.33	Self-determined task order	*Unknown*
				Intervening work	
	Perception	0.44	0.20	Intervening work	*Unknown*
Workload	Vigilance dual task[e]	0.33	0.29	TLX Frustration	Load increase
Fatigue	Vigilance dual task	0.43	0.17	Puzzle completed	Slow speed first
Workload	N-Back task[f]	0.98	0.62	Arithmetic flexibility	2-back to 3-back
				TLX Performance	TLX Temporal demand
				TLX Effort	
				TLX Frustration	
				Inflexibility[g]	
				Monitoring	
Fatigue	N-Back task	0.47	0.37	Work done	Algebra flexibility
				2–3 back load shift	
Workload	Vigilance[h], miss rates	0.39	0.11	Field dependence	Load direction
				Anxiety	Speed
				Irresolute	
	Vigilance, false alarms	0.44	0.04	Anxiety	*Unknown*
				Inflexible	
				Irresolute	

(continued)

Table 8.1 (continued)

Model	Type of task	R^2 Cusp	R^2 Linear[a]	Bifurcation	Asymmetry
Fatigue	Vigilance, miss rates	0.26	0.39	Puzzle completed	*Unknown*
				Working in pairs	
				GSR group	
	Vigilance, false alarms	0.35	0.02	Working in pairs	*Unknown*
				GSR group	
Workload	Financial, optimizing	0.39	0.36	Conscientiousness	Speed condition
				Impulsivity	Load condition
	5 Blocks separately[i]	0.46	0.32	Frustration	Speed
				Conscientiousness	
				Impulsivity	
				Field dependence	
	Financial, risk-taking	0.25	0.25	Work ethic	Load condition
				Field dependence	
	5 Blocks separately	0.28	0.23	Work ethic	speed
				Conscientiousness	
				Impulsivity	
Fatigue	Financial optimizing	0.56	0.24	Speed condition	Field dependence
				Work done	
	5 Blocks separately	0.24	0.21	Work done	Frustration
					Conscientiousness
					Anagrams
					Field dependence
					Impulsivity
	Financial, risk-taking	0.44	0.27	Speed condition	Field dependence
				Work done	Anagrams
	5 Blocks separately	0.35	0.19	Work done	*Unknown*
Summary	**Ave. all models above**	**0.44**	**0.28**		

[a]Pre-post model was the strongest challenger in most cases
[b]Guastello et al. (2012a)
[c]Guastello et al. (2012b)
[d]Guastello et al. (2013)
[e]Guastello et al. (2014). Participants monitored a building security camera, for which the event rates either increased or decreased. The events were nighttime scenarios. The secondary task was to complete a jigsaw puzzle
[f]Guastello et al. (2015)
[g]Inflexibility, monitoring, and irresolute versus decisive are coping styles introduced by Cantwell and Moore (1996)
[h]Guastello et al. (2014). This was also a dual task with a jigsaw puzzle. The events were nighttime scenarios. Participants either worked alone, worked in pairs, or worked in pairs, or worked in pairs while wearing electrodermal response sensors
[i]Average values from four comparisons for stimulus blocks 1 vs 2, 3, 4, and 5 assessed separately

of fatigue, or vice versa. It is a challenge to experimental design to contrive a range of task conditions that is wide enough to cover the full range of cusp dynamics that are thought to underlie the workload and fatigue processes. R^2 for the cusp increases, and improves prediction over the best alternative linear model, to the extent that the full response surface, especially around the bifurcation manifold, is covered.

In the case of the financial decision making task, the fatigue manipulations had a more pronounced effect on performance than the workload manipulations. The block-by-block analyses showed that all four cusp effects were strongest in the transition between blocks 1 and 2, smoothed out over blocks 3 and 4, and picked up again at block 5 (Table 3.10). This pattern suggested that a coping mechanism or acclimation was setting in, but further disruptions occurred when they reached the level of block 5. Participants also had worked longer by the time they reached block 5. Because fatigue would have contributed to the performance changes also, it was necessary to use and interpret the two cusp models for workload and fatigue simultaneously.

The highly variable levels of performance associated with fatigue was very pronounced toward the end of block 6 when the participants were approaching a total of 90 min on task (at the 15-s stimulus pace). The effect in block was the same for those were on task for 45 min working at the fastest pace (7.5 s per stimulus).

The cusp dynamics of workload and fatigue affected risk taking to approximately the same extent as they did for optimizing. It is not clear whether issues of risk or uncertainty could have been operating in more subtle ways in other types of cognitive tasks that were studied previously. This experiment was the first, however, to separate the two processes deliberately.

8.2 Individual Differences

The two cusp models contain provisions for individual differences that correspond to the control parameter for elasticity-rigidity in the workload model and compensatory abilities in the fatigue model. On the one hand it appears that different variables become active in different experiments depending on the nature of the task. Anxiety, for instance only seems to become active if the task involves interactions with other people. On the other hand, it is not yet possible to put together a clear-cut set of contingencies of what to expect in each type of task because not all the variables appearing in Table 8.1 were tested at the same time. In fact we did not think of them all at the same time; new hypotheses for control variables were tested as new ideas surfaced. There was also a limitation as to how many variables and research measurements could be given in an experiment because of limits on the participants' time.

In the particular case of this financial decision task, three variables stood out as being particularly consistent – conscientiousness, field independence, and anagrams. Conscientiousness is a personality trait that can be measured and interpreted in a broad sense that is consistent with the five factor model of personality traits (McCrae and Costa 1985) or in a narrower sense that is consistent with the 16-factor theory (Cattell et al. 1970). The essential between the two views is that the narrow definition separates the core construct of conscientiousness – attention to details and following rules of different sorts – from another narrow construct, self-control versus impulsivity. The trait self-control conveys an element of rigidity that could predispose the individual to catastrophic shifts in performance if stress demands become too strong. Impulsivity implies some amount of spontaneity in the spirit of "let's try something new and see what happens, even though it is not in the plan." A tendency toward immediate self-gratification is part of the trait. Impulsivity in this task context seemed to favor more risky decisions that might or might not pay off. When the broad and narrow scales were tested in the cusp models, there was a consistent configuration of positive conscientiousness and negative self-control (impulsivity) favoring the high-bifurcation end of the cusp response surface of the workload model. The two narrow traits are obviously working at crossed purposes. It is possible for a person to think rigidly in one sense, but volatilely in another. In light of these findings, it is tempting to digress into a critique of the five factor model as whole, but that has been done relatively recently elsewhere (Guastello 2009; Guastello et al. 2014a, 2015a).

Field independence is a relative newcomer to the cognitive workload and fatigue project, although Stamovlasis and Tsaparlis (2012) have been working with it for a longer period of time in their studies of working memory and varying levels of demand in solving context of chemistry problems. The construct actually has two sources of relevance to the present problem. One is the more obvious tendency to isolate and target information from a background of irrelevant information. The other is the premise that field independent people make greater use of their working memory capacities. The empirical result is that field dependent people are more susceptible to the workload effects with the result that field dependence registers at the high-bifurcation side of the cusp response surface.

The implications of the results for field independence could be lucrative for large-scale brokers and fund managers. Prior to the present study, there was only one obstacle that suggested any connection between field independence and success in the financial industry (Mykytyn 1989). We have now ascertained that field independence is germane to the types of decisions that must be made in the financial industry. Of course, future research should verify this assertion with simpler test validity data that correlates a pre-employment test score with eventual performance on the job. Again the temptation to digress into personnel selection theory and strategy must be avoided here, but Guion (1998) is a comprehensive resource on measurement and statistical issues related to selecting personnel for employment in organizations.

The anagrams test was the third outstanding variable that pertained to financial decision making under conditions of cognitive workload and fatigue. Anagrams represent one form of cognitive ability that is associated with creative thinking and creative potential. The experimental task was an optimizing task that required *convergent* thinking and not the *divergent* thinking that is associated with creative thinking. The point was made in Chap. 2, of course, that non-optimal decisions involve a component of optimization before the necessary decisions (e.g. in a design product) are finalized, but the relationship does not work the other way around: Sometimes it is necessary to turn the creative thinking *off* for a while. The participants in this study were not given any such instruction to turn any mental faculties on or off, nor were they told how to figure an expected outcome from knowledge of valence and utility. The results showed, nonetheless, that the participants who performed better were not high-scorers on the anagrams test; in turn, they were less susceptible to taking risks that were unnecessary in this case.

Perceptions of workload were logically related to more demanding experimental conditions and ability measures. Those with the pertinent abilities did not rate the time pressure as high as others did. Those with the field independent cognitive style reported a higher performance requirement from the task, which means higher ratings of workload overall.

8.3 Performance-Variability Paradox

The folk wisdom is that the best performers are also the most consistent performers. The contrary view from nonlinear dynamical systems theory, however, is that some variability must be retained in order to facilitate new levels of adaptation. The study in Chap. 5 showed that is exactly what happened with the optimizing criterion. The Hurst exponent was the single best predictor of performance, and the relationship was negative: The more variable participants performed better overall.

The results for risk taking worked out a bit differently, which is not surprising because risk taking was not a criterion of performance that would be deliberately encouraged if there were not an optimizing goal in the forefront. Those who took more risks overall were *more* persistent or steady about taking them, but the best optimizers took *fewer* risks overall.

The foregoing summary should be tempered with the broader perspective. Although it is true that the nonlinear perspective holds that some variability is necessary for adaptation, it also recognizes that too much variability indicates a system that is working inefficiently out of control altogether. Previous studies have also shown that relatively lower levels of variability in performance are good; the performers spend only very little time in terrible performance states, if any at all. Studies related to the principle of *optimum* variability were cited in Chap. 6. At this point the managerial mind might adopt a different scale of measurement and say that the amount of variability that is helpful for adaptation does not really matter, that perhaps it is just noise anyway, and that a group of employees are steady performers because they have not had a major disaster in many years. That position might be serviceable for purposes of making simple policies, but to say the variation is just noise deflects the true meaning of the variability – it is an intrinsic dynamic of cognition and performance.

The analyses of variability in Chaps. 5 and 6 uncovered some interesting limits to the Hurst exponent (H), which is ordinarily a good indicator of variability within a range from a stable fixed point attractor, to $1/f$ self-organizing dynamics, Brownian motion or true noise, and oscillators. Although H is supposed to reside between the values of 0 and 1, negative values are possible when the dynamics within the time series involve a bifurcation. Hysteresis around the cusp manifold may look like an irregular oscillation (H approaching 0), but the key word is "irregular." The fluctuations are actually governed by two control parameters and occur between two local stabilities, which is different from a simple one-state limit cycle. The two states and control parameters were already expected from the cusp catastrophe model, so the analyses with the Hurst exponent were another way to illustrate some of the same dynamics. On the other hand, if researchers were starting their explorations into a time series phenomenon, a negative H is not sufficient to support the existence of a cusp catastrophe function; it does, however, offer probable cause for deeper theoretical development.

8.4 The Future of Bounded Rationality

The opportunities for bounded rationality and biases in financial decision making, if not elsewhere as well, have expanded considerably since the initial problems of too much information and not enough time to work through the complexities of a situation and process it. The present study focused on two of the best-known biases in decision making, the reflection effect and overweighting certainty. These biases, we found, were exacerbated by cognitive workload and fatigue, which is more specific than simply saying the effects were heightened by "stress." An improved level of specificity enhances one's ability to control the situation. There was somewhat of a seesaw effect between the two biases when they were viewed over time. Risk taking dropped at first then increased, whereas optimization improved or reduced depending on the level of speed stress. The reflection effect occurred in the cases where both optimization and risk taking took downturns.

As with most reasonable experimental strategies, the present suite of studies held numerous contextual variables constant while manipulating the variables of interest. There are many other possible influences on decision making that compromise rationality that need to be considered in future research on temporal dynamics of decision making, in which complexity or workload issues, learning, and fatigue are likely to be involved. Gärling et al. (2009) and a number of economists introduced several that should be considered further, as follows. They can be categorized as resulting from affect, contagion of affect, discounting the future, multiple utilities, heterogeneous agents, hierarchical decision structures, credit decisions, and the differences between novices and experts.

8.4.1 Affect and Contagion

There is the role of affect: How would a particular outcome make a person *feel*? How would an agent's anticipated mood compare with the agent's mood at present? This type of question might be more related to indulgent consumer behavior that it would to portfolio management, but there is an overlap. Stock traders are known to sell their attractive assets, for which they will realize some profit, and hold on to losers. The thinking is that profits make traders happy, but losses make them feel badly. There is probably another reason for keeping losers, which is that, by not realizing the loss, the apparent profits for the year look better to investors. If the investors are unhappy, however, they churn their investments. The other stakeholders can be more influential on a decision than one's own expected affect. In any case, the decisions that were made in the study were essentially buying decisions. Future research should involve combinations of buying, selling, and intervening levels of profit (price movements) as manipulated variables.

It is one thing for an agent to control his or her own tendencies for affect that taints rationality, but what about the rationality of other agents? It is not uncommon (in this writer's experience) to put together a forecast that is based on the assumption that the other agents will be no more or less rational tomorrow than they are today, only to see that assumption was not true. Agents often overreact to news, and the overreaction is typically more severe with negative news than with positive news (Gärling et al. 2009). The first reactions by agents on 1 day create information for other agents the next day, and the sentiment spreads (Gomes 2015). Add the acceleration of the effect produced by automated trading programs, and we have animal spirits, the madness of crowds, flash crashes, and speculative bubbles. Agents can capitalize on these irrationalities if they act quickly enough, or minimize losses if they wait for markets to readjust. Thus the agent's *sense of timing* is another variable to be considered. Here one can expect that cognitive workload and fatigue dynamics would play a facilitating or compromising role, particularly the time pressure aspect of workload.

8.4.2 Discounting and Multiple Utilities

The investment scenarios presented to the participants in this study did not specify how long the investment would require to meet expectations. There is a bias toward discounting the larger future outcomes in favor of smaller positive returns sooner. The rationality of these choices may depend on how badly the individual needs the payment, perhaps to solve another problem in life. Additionally, it is well-known that investors have different financial goals with respect to wealth accumulation, income, and maintenance of resources for retirement funds. Hence the investors have profiles of risk, return, immediacy concerns, long-range concerns, and uncertainties about how long the retirement period of life is going to last. The very presence of these *heterogeneous agents* makes the predictability of expectancies and probabilities more complex and less certain. Thus time to payoff is another variable that could be built into a future study. The certainty or ambiguity of the expected time for a particular payoff could also be varied.

Discounting factors are particularly problematic in ecological economics where multiple utilities are involved, and the utilities to the individual agent associated with depleting a resource are positive, and the utilities to the collective are negative (Carpenter et al. 1999; Rosser 2001). Profits for the individual agents today, if carried too far, result in no available resources for other agents. Hence we have the classic "tragedy of the commons," collapse of some fisheries in the late 1990s, and persistent concern about global warming, the contributions of carbon emissions, and the impact of warming on different parts of the globe. At the national level of decision making, countries differ in their policies that trade off how much pollution they are willing to accept into their living environments in exchange for profits and economic growth today compared to the livability within their own borders if not the world in the future.

At some level, policy makers are optimizing their own outcomes based on forecasts, and forecasting errors, of future environmental states. The relationships among economic and ecological variables are complex and nonlinear over time and geographic regions, so it is perhaps not a surprise that globally acceptable policies do not exist at present.

Note that the nonlinearities and complexities exist in the problem solving environment of ecological economics. The choices that could be made by economic agents that are similar to the ones participating in the present research do not lend themselves to time series analysis. The agents engage an extensive task of determining and juggling expected outcomes and probabilities to arrive at one decision that is meant to stay in place for an extended period of time, usually followed by sub-decisions of different types that put the primary decision into action. Decisions can be hierarchically structured. Thus there are decision structures that fall outside the scope of the present study in which one agent makes repeated decisions on behalf of self, clients, or stakeholders as a unit.

8.4.3 Credit Decisions

Credit risk is another type of investment that should be evaluation for temporal dynamics. To the banker, the profits come in the form of inherent payments received, and the losses come from loan customers defaulting. To the home loan consumer, there are costs in the form of mortgage payment but not financial gains; the gains exist only in the value of owning and using the property, which is a powerful-enough motive. Speculation in housing is possible, however, which leads to a more general question: How much debt is the investor willing to accept in order to take advantage of an investment opportunity? Corporations make this decision whenever they issue bonds. Stock traders do the same when they buy securities on margin. The expected time to payoff should play a role in their choices.

8.4.4 Novices and Experts

That said, there are differences between relatively naïve undergraduates who participated in this research and professional brokers, fund managers, and policy makers. At the same time, entire industries have been built on the economic decisions of people aged 15–30, so the undergraduate "laboratory rat" is not irrelevant. Thus as one studies decisions that have greater levels of complexity, greater differences between novices and experts become apparent. Experts as a general rule should be able to recognize a decision situation more quickly, ascertain the relevant information used to make it, and execute the cognitive routines more fluidly. Intuition is part of what experts have to offer; they can look at a situation that is ambiguous to novices, and target the right avenues to investigate and narrow down their possible strategies when relevant information is less than complete. Because cognitive workload and fatigue has its primary impact on these functions of working memory, experts should be more immune to workload and fatigue for longer periods of time, all other things being equal.

The foregoing is a long to-do list for future research and unlikely to be completed overnight. The range of potential complexities of decisions is no doubt extensive. Until then cognitive researchers should, hopefully, find that enough has been accomplished to this point to get through the day.

References

Cantwell, R. H., & Moore, P. J. (1996). The development and measurement of individual differences in self-regulatory control and their relationship to academic performance. *Contemporary Educational Psychology, 21*, 500–517.

Carpenter, S. R., Ludwig, D., & Brock, W. A. (1999). Management for eutrophication of lakes subject to potentially irreversible change. *Ecological Applications, 9*, 751–771.

Cattell, R. B., Eber, H. W., & Tatsuoka, M. M. (1970). *Handbook for the sixteen personality factor questionnaire*. Champaign: Institute for Personality and Ability Testing.

Gärling, T., Kirchler, E., Lewis, A., & van Raaij, F. (2009). Psychology, financial decision making, and financial crises. *Psychological Science in the Public Interest, 10*, 1–47.

Gomes, O. (2015). A model of animal spirits via sentiment spreading. *Nonlinear Dynamics, Psychology, and Life Sciences, 19*, 313–343.

Guastello, S. J. (2009). Creativity and personality. In T. Rickards, M. A. Runco, & S. Moger (Eds.), *Routledge companion to creativity* (pp. 267–278). Abington: Routledge.

Guastello, S. J., Boeh, H., Shumaker, C., & Schimmels, M. (2012a). Catastrophe models for cognitive workload and fatigue. *Theoretical Issues in Ergonomics Science, 13*, 586–602.

Guastello, S. J., Boeh, H., Schimmels, M., Gorin, H., Huschen, S., Davis, E., Peters, N. E., Fabisch, M., & Poston, K. (2012b). Cusp catastrophe models for cognitive workload and fatigue in a verbally-cued pictorial memory task. *Human Factors, 54*, 811–825.

Guastello, S. J., Boeh, H., Gorin, H., Huschen, S., Peters, N. E., Fabisch, M., & Poston, K. (2013). Cusp catastrophe models for cognitive workload and fatigue: A comparison of seven task types. *Nonlinear Dynamics, Psychology, and Life Sciences, 17*, 23–47.

Guastello, A. D., Guastello, S. J., & Guastello, D. D. (2014a). Personality trait theory and multitasking performance: Implications for ergonomic design. *Theoretical Issues in Ergonomics Science, 15*, 432–450.

Guastello, S. J., Malon, M., Timm, P., Weinberger, K., Gorin, H., Fabisch, M., & Poston, K. (2014b). Catastrophe models for cognitive workload and fatigue in a vigilance dual-task. *Human Factors, 56*, 737–751.

Guastello, S. J., Malon, M., Shaline, J., Abraham, J., Hilo, M., Krueger, J., McCormack, N., & Sapnu, E. (2014c). *Cognitive workload and fatigue in a vigilance dual task: Miss errors, false alarms, and the impact of wearing biometric sensors while working*. Paper presented to the 24th annual international conference of the Society for Chaos Theory in Psychology & Life Sciences, Milwaukee.

Guastello, S. J., Shircel, A., Malon, M., & Timm, P. (2015a). Individual differences in the experience of cognitive workload. *Theoretical Issues in Ergonomics Science, 16*, 20–52.

Guastello, S. J., Reiter, K., Malon, M., Timm, P., Shircel, A., & Shaline, J. (2015b). Catastrophe models for cognitive workload and fatigue in N-back tasks. *Nonlinear Dynamics, Psychology, and Life Sciences, 19*, 173–200.

Guion, R. M. (1998). *Assessment, measurement, and prediction for personnel decisions*. Mahwah: Lawrence Erlbaum Associates.

McCrae, R. R., & Costa, P. T., Jr. (1985). Updating Norman's "adequate taxonomy:" Intelligence and personality dimensions in natural language questionnaires. *Journal of Personality and Social Psychology, 49*, 710–721.

Mykytyn, P. P., Jr. (1989). Group embedded figures test (GEFT): Individual differences, performance, and learning effects. *Educational and Psychological Measurement, 49*, 951–959.

Rosser, J. B., Jr. (2001). Complex ecological-economic dynamics and environmental policy. *Ecological Economics, 37*, 23–37.

Stamovlasis, D., & Tsaparlis, G. (2012). Applying catastrophe theory to an information-processing model of problem solving in science education. *Science Education, 96*, 392–410.

Index

S.J. Guastello (ed.), *Cognitive Workload and Fatigue in Financial Decision Making*, Evolutionary Economics and Social Complexity Science 13,
DOI 10.1007/978-4-431-55312-0

The manufacturer's authorised representative in the EU is Springer
Nature Customer Service Centre GmbH, Europaplatz 3, 69115 Heidelberg,
Germany. If you have any concerns regarding our products, please
contact ProductSafety@springernature.com

Printed and bound by CPI Group (UK) Ltd, Croydon, CR0 4YY
27/09/2026
02223591-0002